D1157008

It Is Easier to Succeed Than to Fail

It Is Easier to Succeed Than to Fail

Ralph W. O'Farrell

Parker Publishing Company, Inc.
West Nyack, N. Y.

PARKER PUBLISHING COMPANY, INC.

West Nyack, N. Y.

Library of Congress
Catalog Card Number: 66-11598

PRINTED IN THE UNITED STATES OF AMERICA

50652—B&P

To the friendliest person I ever met . . .

my Mother

You *Can* Succeed . . .
It's Easier Than You Think

The theme of this book may strike you as a bit strange. After all, isn't it a lot easier to fail at something than to be successful? Success takes effort; success takes unique qualities that only a few have; and yes, success takes a good helping of luck, too. To fail, on the other hand, requires none of these. Is it *really* easier to succeed than to fail?

This book will convince you that success is far easier. Success of any kind, no matter what it is you may be after. No one wants to fail. Every one of us desires personal, business, professional, financial, and social success. The goal of success is something each of us wants. It should certainly be much easier to achieve something you want, and to avoid something you don't want. No one really wants to fail in anything. So why not do what you want and do what is easier . . . be successful.

It Is Easier to Succeed Than to Fail points up the reasons success is easier, and gives you sound ideas and approaches you can use to achieve the success you want in your life. It shows you that within every person are certain innate qualities and abilities that can be used to develop the total personal power that leads to success—qualities such as enthusiasm, individuality, determination, flexibility, confidence, and leadership, that make the road to successful achievement seem easy.

Within the 20 chapters of this book you will find the philosophy, the technique, the system that every successful and happy person uses to build the foundation for a life of achievement that is the envy of those who, deliberately or unknowingly, follow the hard and dusty road to failure and disappointment. Follow the high road, the fast road, the easy road, and you cannot help but make your dreams and desires come true, for it really is much easier to succeed than to fail.

Contents

1

How to Get Out the Hidden Talents and Possibilities Hammering and Storming Within You

YOU—AND THE THINGS BOTTLED UP WITHIN YOU

The day you were born you became an individual—an individual with many undeveloped talents and many hidden abilities. You could not walk; you could not talk; but you were an individual unlike any other person in the world.

No other baby was born at that time of the same mother and father, at the same place, having the same fingerprints.

Now, if you were the usual type of baby, you cried a lot that first year, and only your mother and father could interpret your mumbling as, "ello, drand pa" and "bye . . . bye . . . an berie."

Unless you were a very unusual baby or your father was a photographer, you failed to make a single dime the first six years of your life. But you *were* developing into the YOU that you are today.

First, you were taught how to crawl, then to walk. Then you learned to talk. By this time, your personality and your individuality were being formed and affected by the things you came in contact with—the playmates in your neighborhood, your teachers at school, and your family at home.

The YOU that you now are is not always the real you or the best you. Nearly everyone has undeveloped abilities. Many times they are unknown. Many times they bounce around within the person for a lifetime, never to be developed or enjoyed.

To those who are willing to spend a little time and effort to become a better and more successful "Individual," a loose-leaf notebook will be very helpful. As you browse through these chapters, you will be asked to make notes. When you finish, you will have a concise analysis of yourself—with suggestions, ideas, and an easy-to-follow program that could make you a better individual 24 hours a day.

In the fast-changing world in which we live the ability to be an individual becomes more important every day. Each year, "Big Corporations" look over the crop of college graduates, and the individual who stands out from the pack is usually selected. Although the school record is important, there are many with excellent scholastic records in the same group. So, the interviewer is looking for that little difference that sets a person apart.

It could be his handshake and his personable smile. It might be the way he is dressed and his mannerisms. The tone of his voice, along with a friendly twinkle in his eyes, could make the difference. But, in the end, it is the individual who has recognized and developed those hidden talents and personality traits that have stormed and hammered within him—that made the difference.

Scientists tell us that we are only using a small portion of our brain—that we have no conception of the capacity of this gray matter with its hidden potentialities. In addition to utilizing only a small part of this wonderful storeroom of knowledge, we actually know very little about "How to develop the unused part."

It may take thousands of years for us to reach the half-way mark. Most of us cannot wait that long. In the meantime, we have undeveloped talents and abilities hammering and storming within us—endeavoring to get out and express themselves. These we *can* do something about.

What can be done about these talents and abilities bouncing around within you—and how it can be done by you as an Individual—will be revealed to you as you read *It Is Easier to Succeed Than to Fail.* On your part, it will require the following:

1. Time
2. Effort
3. Thought
4. A Program

First, I think we should establish a few ground rules and understandings. We have all read many times . . .

- You can be anything you want to be.
- How to make everyone simply go crazy about you.
- How to make everyone stand perfectly still with mouth open when you speak, and so forth.

Now, we do not have to be very smart to know that to accept these sayings in their full meaning is ridiculous. I, for one, could never be an opera singer or a tight-rope walker or play tackle on the New York Giants Football Team. And—if the truth were really known—I doubt very much if I could hold a job as a fast package wrapper in a large department store.

But, I can, and you can, do most of the things we want to do within our own capacity—and our own capacity is much greater than most of us realize.

Having hidden abilities and talents is one thing—getting them out and developing them is something else. One of the most essential *firsts* is to recognize these potential qualities. If it is difficult for you to realize that you have them, try and observe and recognize them in other people, particularly successful individuals and individuals you like.

If you will make a note of all the things you like and admire in other people, you will generally find that if you, yourself, develop these same traits, you too will be successful and liked.

Recently, a young executive group raised this question:

> Although we read and read about how to succeed, how to win friends, how to do this, and how to do that, a week later all the things we have read are

just so many words. What we would like is a list of the 25 most important abilities we have within us, so we could check these against our daily problems and our progress in our community—and at work.

Out of 50 suggested important abilities, these 25 were selected:

THE ABILITY TO:

1. Call on your best personality when needed.
2. Deal with all types of people.
3. Recognize problems quickly, and to be able to formulate a program without delay.
4. Know when and how to compromise, and still get the most in return for yourself.
5. Develop the kind of confidence that will overcome fear.
6. Be able to think clearly and thoroughly without prejudice.
7. Be able to create enthusiasm.
8. Be able to understand other people's viewpoints when they differ with yours.
9. Be able to accept set-backs, and to profit by your experience and failures when you start over again.
10. Have a set program of making written notes of your ideas, problems, mistakes, and your goals; and have the courage to evaluate, change, and keep these up to date.
11. Be able to avoid common and apparent mistakes.
12. Be able to develop your own individuality that you will be proud of—and others will like.

13. Be tactful under difficult circumstances and situations.
14. Be able to be friendly in unfriendly surroundings.
15. Check out your ideas and have the tenacity to double-check them.
16. Accept the things you cannot change and have the courage to change the things that should be changed.
17. Be able to recognize values and ideas.
18. Be flexible under any circumstances.
19. Be able to work with all types of people and personalities.
20. Speak effectively before any group or gathering.
21. Be able to accept responsibility along with authority.
22. Know how and when to expend the necessary energy to accomplish what has to be accomplished.
23. Have the ability to know what work should be detailed to others and the "know-how" to have the people handling the details wanting to do a good job for you.
24. Be able to work with others as a teammate.
25. Be a leader when called upon—a leader with a purpose, who not only can lead, but who can guide and counsel.

Six months later, the young executive group posed another question.

> Could we be given a complete example of how some ordinary person had an idea—preferably an idea about moving ahead in a fairly large corporation—and how he checked out this idea? Then show how he formulated a program to carry this out, how he created his own enthusiasm. We want to see detailed steps from beginning to end.

The group felt that if this could be done, that this example would be more helpful than a set of instructions that never seemed to fit the situation when it arose—that it would also stimulate individual thinking in checking out the 25-point outline.

HOW ONE MAN DEALT WITH HIS HAMMERING AND STORMING TALENTS

John Franklin had been a very successful salesman, but for years he had had the burning desire to get into administrative or personnel work. This he studied for in college; but having married young, he took the first job that came along. He planned to move into his selected field when he had saved a little money and the opportunity presented itself. Twenty years later, although he had tried, he just could not seem to break through the barrier that separated the sales force from the inner office.

Before we start the story of John Franklin, let's take a close look at him. He was a very personable gentleman, with a warm, disarming smile. He had enthusiasm, courage, and worked well with others. Above all, he was a company man. But, within him, he had storming and hammering abilities that wanted to get out.

During the past five years, John became aware of competing companies merging—of the trend of big companies to buy out small companies, of companies who were noted for a certain product diversifying by buying out companies who produced a related product. Then, he heard that his company had decided to build a plant in Puerto Rico. He knew that certain top personnel would be selected to take over. The company would move into the plant in about 18 months. In about a year, the personnel selected would start a 6-month training program. John had spent some time in Puerto Rico during the war and liked it.

John had an IDEA. It was only an idea, but the more he thought about it, the more it hammered within him. Why couldn't he be one of those selected to go to Puerto Rico?

First, he should *check out his idea.* This he did. He checked it out with his wife. Since this would mean moving to San Juan, she was the most important person to approve or disapprove the move.

The Franklins had two children: a daughter who was married and a son who had finished college and who was finishing up his stretch in the army. It was agreed that the family ties were not a problem.

Second, how would they feel about starting life over in new surroundings without friends? They felt that John's not having to travel and the climate would offset this disadvantage. Furthermore, they both felt, having moved several times in the last five years, they could adapt themselves to almost any surroundings. Besides, both liked people and moved very well in all circles. John's idea was a stimulating challenge!

Third, John double-checked to find out all he could about why the company was making this move. Then, he began to formulate a program—not merely an IDEA in his head, but a complete program.

Fourth, he wanted to find out for himself why the company was building a large plant in San Juan. He found out that Tax Research Institute, Inc. on Fifth Avenue in New York had written a Tax Planning Report entitled *Puerto Rican Tax Holiday Continues to Be Important*. John sent for this report and found

> That Puerto Rico provides opportunities to American Business which cannot be duplicated on the Mainland or in other countries. A combination of U.S. and Puerto Rican tax law provisions make it possible to earn income from a Puerto Rican operation completely tax free.

John also read that, besides the company getting tax advantages, he also would be given tax advantages. He checked again and found that his company had met certain qualifications entitling the company to possibly a 10-year operation without paying any income tax at all—either to Puerto Rico or to the United States.

John was now ready for a step-by-step program. Both he and his wife had taken Spanish in school, but this was far from being a conversational language between them. Besides, they had studied Castilian Spanish, and the Spanish spoken in Puerto Rico was slightly different. Since John was on the road a good deal of the time, he could not very well go to school. So they set upon another plan.

Mrs. Franklin bought the records and instructions entitled *Living Spanish.* Next, she asked a young Puerto Rican waiter at their country club who spoke excellent English as well as Spanish to check the records as to the difference in the pronunciation between Castilian Spanish and the Puerto Rican Spanish.

She then began to put these lessons on their portable tape recorder, translating the words and sayings into English, then into Spanish, then back to English. Since John traveled quite a bit, it was thought advisable to get another portable tape recorder. In this way, John could play these lessons over and over again as he traveled from city to city.

The Franklins next decided to speak nothing but Spanish in their home. Then they sent for a Puerto Rican newspaper to be mailed to them every week. With the aid of their friend, the young Puerto Rican waiter, they both progressed rapidly.

While they were learning Spanish, the Franklins decided they would learn something about the history and the people of Puerto Rico. They sent for an article entitled, "San Juan National Historic Site," put out by the United States Department of the Interior. Through their young Puerto Rican, they were able to secure some literature on the problems in Puerto Rico, the laws, educational and housing problems, etc.

At the end of three months, the Franklins were speaking and reading Spanish in understandable style.

Mrs. Franklin began to reduce their program and plans to writing. This they checked and rechecked.

John had a three weeks' vacation coming. It was only natural that the Franklins spend their vacation in Puerto Rico. They worked out their program for the trip. Here it is in outline form:

1. Take along tape recorder. Re-listen to Spanish lessons. Make recordings of conversations with Puerto Ricans.
2. Visit site where plant is to be built.
3. Contact the manager or executive officer of at least ten companies who have moved to Puerto Rico and qualified under the Industrial Incentive Act. Find out the following:
   a. Problems in hiring.
   b. Study union activities.
   c. Problems with employees.
   d. Study the records of the Puerto Rican employee as to productivity in comparison to the American.
   e. Get copies of all laws affecting employment.
   f. Study problems in plant security, pilfering, etc.
   g. Try to get important comments by an executive on tape.
   h. Study and reduce to writing, or put on tape, the following:
      Housing, transportation, education facilities, available. Help—including office help, factory, shipping, trucking, etc. Also check golf courses, night clubs, hotel accommodations, etc.

In addition to completing the entire schedule, John had a conference with two union officials in regard to policy of organizing workers. It included contract problems with employers and a discussion of the wage scale and other benefits. (*Note:* In all conferences with business executives and union officials, John at no time disclosed any information about his company—its name or the fact it planned on opening a branch in Puerto Rico. He merely introduced himself and informed the people he interviewed that he was writing an article on American business operations in San Juan—which of course he was doing.)

Speaking pretty good Spanish helped him to a great extent. On one occasion, while interviewing a top executive of a firm that had located in Pureto Rico four years ago, he found that the manager had died the week before. The president, who had flown down from New York, was so impressed with John's knowledge of business operations in San Juan, plus his ability to talk to and understand his foreman who spoke only a few words in English, that he offered him the job as manager. John advised the president he would need three months before he could give him a firm answer. To his surprise, the president agreed to keep the job open for that period of time.

Before the Franklins left Puerto Rico, John taped an interview with the traffic manager of a large corporation who told him how in the last year the company had worked out a transportation idea wherein they could pack an entire box car right in the plant, take it by truck to the dock, then by barge to Mobile, Alabama, and then by "piggy-back" to their warehouse in Chicago. The entire package unit was delivered to Chicago cheaper than the unit could be produced and packaged in Chicago, where the company had a large plant. This, plus the tax advantage, made the Puerto Rican operation very profitable.

The last thing John did before flying back was to make out a complete list of all the products his company manufactured and made a tape on how these items would be pronounced in Spanish by the people in San Juan.

It took over a month for the Franklins to reduce all their findings to outline form, and to delete, cut, and organize the tape recordings. Three times John rewrote his outline, condensing it, setting it up under different titles and headings, and finally completing it with an index.

It was now seven months since the idea hit john—the idea that just maybe he could be selected as one of the executives to go to Puerto Rico.

For over a week, he thought over various ways of presenting his findings to management. Then he made his decision.

First, he went to his boss, the person in charge of sales. But, before going, he thought out his approach in detail. He put his short talk on tape and listened to himself talking to his boss. He didn't quite like what he heard, and he made some changes and re-taped it again. It was better, but not quite what he wanted to hear. The third time it pleased him.

His pitch to the head of the sales department was

quite simple. He had been very interested in locating in Puerto Rico for some time. Both he and his wife had made a study of the language, the people, and American business locating there. He had been offered a job there; but before deciding definitely on the offer, he would like to talk to the person in charge of the new plant in San Juan. A meeting was arranged.

The executive vice president was so impressed with John's presentation, the tape recordings, and his unusual knowledge about operations in Puerto Rico, plus his ability to speak the native tongue, that he asked him to make a presentation with his recordings before the board of directors.

When John was selected as the manager of the new plant in San Juan, the buzzing around the inner office was, "Boy, I wonder where he got the 'clout' to get that position. He must know someone real big at the top—or, say, maybe he had something on someone."

As the Young Executive group analyzed the story of John Franklin, here is what they noted—

At first, John had only an idea. But he began to work it out immediately.

He had tried before, but he was not afraid to start over again.

He checked out his idea. Then he double-checked it.

He knew that for years things had been storming and hammering within him. This could be the time to get them out.

He created enthusiasm by picturing the ultimate goal.

He put his plan down in writing.

He added to his program as new ideas appeared.
He used both the tape recorder and his notes to prepare his final presentation.
He recognized the value of his wife's ability in working out the details of the program from beginning to end.
He dared to be different.
He never got lost in details or side-tracked down unrelated alleys.
He used the best part of his personality in dealing with everyone who contributed to the data he presented.
He gathered facts and fit them in their proper place.
He had confidence in himself and the program he formulated.
He made decisions when decisions had to be made.
He was an individual from start to finish.

DO NOT BE AFRAID TO START OVER

The fact that in the past you have felt that you had some undeveloped or hidden abilities, and that you made a real effort to better yourself and failed, should not stop you from formulating a new program for the future.

Before starting a new program, let's take a good look at our last effort. Let's be honest and realistic with ourselves.

Did we have a well-defined outline or merely an idea?
Were we reaching for something within our capacity or something out in left field?

Did we want to accomplish it badly enough to give it a real try, or merely dream of an accomplishment?

Regardless of what your answers are, it should not deter you from starting over again. If you want to read about a few gentlemen who were not afraid to start over after they failed and failed again, well, read the life of Abraham Lincoln or our present-day, successful television personality and band leader, Lawrence Welk. If you read their life histories, you will find that for a long time it looked as though they were failures. But, they never quit trying.

If you are starting over in something that you did not quite finish or something you finished with no results, or if you are making a renewed effort in something a little different, the basic rules are the same.

First, check out your idea. Do you feel that you have that something within you that has possibilities that you have never developed or that you never had time to develop? Are you willing to spend a little time and effort in your own behalf? If so, let's start with a written outline of our idea of what you would like to accomplish. When you decide to do something about this idea, you have started to plunge ahead.

The world is full of "Some day I'm going to" people. Most of these individuals do not have something storming and hammering within them. At their best, they have only a slight rustling, and this rustling will quiet down to a faint murmer at the sight of an easychair.

Let's get out of that "Some day I'm going to" class by starting now.

If you need help in planning your outline, do not be afraid to seek help. Discuss your plans with people who know you and with people who are well-informed in the field where your ultimate goal is located. Accept constructive criticism. Be willing to alter your program, keeping your ultimate goal in mind.

Do not feel that starting over again is repatching an old failure—proper mental attitude is a must. Bring out your sense of humor when you find you are not quite making the progress you planned. Some people have the ability to make a game out of the program they have formulated. You could almost say they play and smile their way into success.

Whether it be learning a language, developing the ability to speak effectively before large gatherings, or merely how to control your temper, *don't bog yourself down by being too serious.*

If you find that starting over by yourself is difficult, find someone who would like to accomplish the same thing. Set up a "do it together" program. Above all, be willing to start over again when things start running astray. Use your experiences and pitfalls as guides in setting up your new program.

YOU MUST THINK OF YOURSELF AS IMPORTANT

Remember there is quite a bit of difference between, "Thinking of yourself as important" and *acting* important.

You owe it to your family, your associates at work,

and to yourself to feel important. Without this feeling, it is most difficult to create enthusiasm, to feel needed, to have the necessary confidence that leads to accomplishments.

We have all met people who act very important. It is possible that they do not feel important at all. That is why they feel it is necessary to create the atmosphere of importance. But this atmosphere is often resented.

When you have abilities storming within you and trying to get out—trying to express themselves—unless you think of yourself as important, you will exert very little effort to do anything about them.

At a family dinner one night, the grandfather was heard to remark, "Guess I'm not important any more. Jim didn't call me this year to help him plant his garden." The little seven-year-old grandson spoke up. "Yes you are. You're important, Grandpa. Our Sunday-school teacher told us that God thinks we're all important. And if God thinks you're important, you 'gotta' be important."

I am asked many times—How do you get to feeling important? The answer is simple, but is not always easy to do.

To have the feeling and to think of yourself as important, you must have accomplished something, no matter how small. You must think that you are needed by someone. You must have the feeling of being liked —of contributing something. You must have the feeling of being able to assist others, of playing an important part in your community, in your church, or at work.

If each of us will only stop and think, we will find

that we can do something a little better, with a little less effort than the other fellow. Remember, at some time or another we all need help. Being able to be helpful to the other person, as well as ourselves, is the formula to thinking of ourselves as important.

When you have the feeling of being needed, when you think of yourself as important, you are well on the way to creating the necessary desire for formulating a program to get out and develop some of those hidden talents and abilities that are hammering within you.

DO NO REACH FOR THE IMPOSSIBLE

Trying to keep up with the Joneses who are too far ahead of you and reaching for the impossible are two things that can create tension, anxiety, and frustration. You only have to read what medical science feels about these three dragons of modern times to know that if you plan on leading a normal and successful life in this fast tempo of modern business, these Three Dragons have got to go.

If Jack Dempsey had wanted to be a jockey and the famous Eddie Arcaro had a burning desire to be the heavyweight champion of the world, I am sure we would have had two frustrated gentlemen instead of two great champions.

How can each of us tell what is the impossible? This again is a decision for each individual. We do have guides and rules to help us. We also must realize that there are many talents and abilities that rest on the borderline.

I have always found it wise when I felt that something was a bit out of reach—something resting between the improbable and the impossible—to talk it over with someone who knew a little more about what I was trying to reach than I did. I usually talked it over with three or four people first, and then myself.

I weighed the effort I must expend—the set-backs I would encounter. I then compared them with the advantages and the "up-lifting" feeling I would get if I succeeded. I generally decided that it was within reach and gave it a good try. I always remembered my number-one MUST—*formulate a complete plan and work from a written program.*

A friend of mine used to tell a story about "Some people do not know when they are reaching for the impossible."

It seems that a couple of friends attended a cocktail party, and near the end, John fell out of the third story window but fortunately landed on the canopy over the main entrance. When Fred, his pal, visited him in the hospital the next morning, John had only one question, "What happened to me last night?"

"Well," said Fred a bit sheepishly, "it was about three o'clock; and, well, we both were feeling no pain. You walked over to the window and said, 'I think I'll get a bit of air and fly around the block.' Well, you climbed up on the window sill, and stretching out your arms—jumped!"

"But, Fred," John pleaded, "why in the world didn't you stop me? You knew I couldn't fly around the block—that's impossible."

"Well, yes, I suppose I did know it was impossible;

but you know, right at that moment when you climbed up on the windowsill and stretched out your arms—I thought you could."

EVEN DAYDREAMS CAN COME TRUE

There is a difference between daydreams engendering an idea and the idea developing into a reality, and daydreaming merely to avoid facing a reality.

Several years ago the Employers' Association of Greater Chicago sent out a pamphlet entitled, *If Everyone Had a Million Dollars.* Surely all of us at one time or another have dreamed about having a million dollars. The thought about everyone having a million dollars seemed to be the answer to most of our problems. Poverty and slum areas would be eliminated; there would be plenty of money for research, hospitals, schools, roads. But, wait a minute; this is the kind of daydream we all have at times to get away from the reality of making a living. With everyone having a million dollars, this is what happened. The milkman didn't show up the next morning. The corner drugstore failed to open. There was no newspaper on the front lawn. The taxicabs went into hiding, and the busses didn't run. Why should all this happen? Everybody had a million dollars and no one would work.

But there is a kind of daydreaming that can lead to accomplishments—like thinking of things you would like to own and developing a plan how to obtain them. Here are some typical daydreams that can lead to accomplishments:

Feeling some of the hidden potentialities you have within you and dreaming about what you can do to get them out.

Picturing how you will handle a certain ticklish situation that is bound to arise.

Planning ahead for next week, next month, and next year.

Seeing yourself playing a new role at the office and moving up a step closer to top management.

Dreaming about that fishing trip and that golf game that will give you that much needed bit of relaxation from the daily grind and the fast tempo of modern business.

Daydreaming should not be done when you are supposed to be working. This could give you a guilt complex, and destroy that enthusiasm that you needed to get past the dreaming stage.

I know an Executive who does most of his daydreaming when he is getting a haircut, riding the train to and from work, or relaxing in a warm tub bath before retiring.

If you have decided to set up a loose-leaf notebook as you browse through this book, do the following:

- On the first page write or type—*I will try to enter all important ideas and thoughts here in outline form. I will take a look at what I wrote at the end of each week to see if I want to make any changes or make any additions.*

• On page two write—*Talents and abilities I feel I have hidden within me.*

• On page three write—*Talents and abilities I like in other people.*

• On page four write—*Failings and faults I feel I have that hinder me in business and in dealing with other people.*

• On page five write—*The kind of personality I would like to develop.*

• On page six write—*Things I will make an effort to accomplish.*

Since each of us is a distinct individual, I will not attempt to tell you what to enter on these pages. However, make your entries as you read chapter by chapter. Be both analytical and honest with yourself.

POINTS TO REMEMBER ABOUT GETTING OUT YOUR HIDDEN TALENTS AND ABILITIES

- You are an *individual;* and it is this individuality that separates you from the crowd. Learn to capitalize on it.

- You only use a small portion of your brain. To free your hidden talents, you must employ (1) Time, (2) Effort, (3) Thought, (4) a Program.

- To recognize potential talents and abilities in yourself, recognize them first in other people.

- Review repeatedly the 25-point outline of important abilities.
- Use the John Franklin case-history as a guide and inspiration.
- Never be afraid to start over, but be realistic and honest with yourself.
- Think of yourself as important, but don't be too serious about yourself.
- Do not reach for the impossible.
- Formulate a complete plan and work from a written program. Keep a notebook in the manner suggested in Chapter 1.
- Examine your daydreams to see if they are a source of inspiration for you or if they are actually hindering the expression of your talents.

2

Be An Individual That You and Your Friends Like

THE YOU THAT OTHER PEOPLE SEE

Most of us do not know how we look, how we sound, or how our general attitude affects other people.

The first time a person hears his or her voice on a recording, he generally looks up with amazement—"That's me?" he says, "I sound like that?" But the fact is, we have been listening to our own voices all our lives, and never realized how we sound. It also is not unusual for a person to be showing a group picture and remark, "It's pretty good of everyone but me." Or a husband showing a picture of himself and his wife might say "Isn't she pretty; but did you ever see a worse picture of me?"

If we stop and realize that we do not know how we look and sound to other people, it is only natural that we are often not aware how we affect these individuals by what we say, by the tone of our voice, and our expressions and mannerisms.

Before we start to determine the type of individual each of us would like to be, let's for the time being forget the "I know me" attitude that most of us have, take a look at a few facts, and ask ourselves a few questions.

- Have you ever seen yourself when you are asleep?
- Have you ever had a good look at yourself when you are mad and "really telling someone off"?
- Do you ever remember seeing yourself when you were happy or telling a joke?
- What about when you are embarrassed or caught off-guard?
- How do you think you look when you are criticizing someone, or when someone is criticizing you?
- How do you think you look and speak after the third cocktail? After the fifth? After . . .? Oh, well, each of us will have to figure this out for ourselves as individuals.

However, the answer to these and other similar questions constitutes the YOU as seen by other people.

I remember being at a cocktail party one evening where a certain individual insisted upon speaking with authority on every subject that came up for discussion. Near the end of the evening, someone whispered in my ear, "He would have to be 150 years old to know all he thinks he knows."

I am sure this well-informed individual who had something to say on every subject never realized the impression he was making. Whether he was an individual that he himself liked, or was merely trying to be an individual that he thought other people would like, I really cannot tell. But when he left the party, he was a worn-out person. He could have—with a little timing, a little more listening, a dash of humor, a sprinkle of humility, a smile of approval now and then—been an individual that his friends liked; and realizing that, he could have possibly been an individual that he himself liked.

(NOTE: If you have set up a loose-leaf notebook, start page seven. Entitle it—*Things I Learn About Myself.* As you browse through the book, make notes on this page of the things you learn about yourself, both good and bad. If you are not sure whether a certain trait is a part of you, if you are in doubt, enter it anyway and put a question mark behind it. It is possible, if you are honest in your appraisals, that it will either take form or disappear.)

EVERYONE LIKES A FRIENDLY PERSON

The wag of a little dog's tail, the grin of a freckle-faced boy, the assuring smile of a nurse—these are the things that can brighten the day or light up a room.

It is difficult for some people to be friendly. First, by nature, they were not gifted with a natural friendliness. Second, they do not know when they are unfriendly. Third, the effort they must put forth to be friendly—well, at times, it just doesn't seem to be worth the effort.

But friendliness is the most disarming weapon that any individual can possess. The friendliest person I ever met was my mother. During her last illness, a priest was making the rounds in the hospital and stopped by to say hello. He had been ill, and it was not too easy for him to smile or be overly friendly. As he came through the door, my mother greeted him with, "Father, if you are coming in here with a long, sour look on your face, you can just stay out of here." This was at 3 P.M. Mother died three hours later.

I used to say about mother, "She seems to be in business for everyone but herself." I remember that there was a period when mother seemed to be buying toothbrushes every other day. These toothbrushes never seemed to turn up around the house. So one day I said, "Mother, what goes with those toothbrushes? You keep buying them, but where do they go?"

"Ralph," she said, "There is a real poor family living down on Third Street, and their name is Rose. There's father and mother and ten children; and, you know, they don't have their own toothbrushes. So I found out their names, and when I get an extra 39 cents I buy one, put a name on it, and send it to them."

She then looked at me with that friendly smile of hers and said, "I only have two more to go."

Several years later when mother was in the hospital, I was looking over her "get well" cards. I noticed a very plain card that read, "To a most marvelous Lady," signed, "A Dozen Roses."

MAKE A NOTE OF WHAT YOU LIKE IN OTHER PEOPLE

Most of us do not stop to analyze why we like certain people or why we do not particularly care for others. However, if you will, pause here and select three individuals you like very well, and three you could well get along without.

a. Study each individual, his personality, abilities, etc.
b. Make two lists: one noting the things you feel make you like each of your three favorite friends, and one noting the traits that you feel make you dislike the other three.
c. Review your two lists. How many things have you noted on list one that you feel could help you be more friendly? Then take a good look at list number two. Do you see any personality traits that are a part of you which tend to make you an unfriendly person?
d. Review this list every month for three months. See how many traits you can adopt on list one, and how many you can cross out on list two.

THE TELEPHONE CAN BE YOUR FRIEND OR YOUR ENEMY

Consider the telephone. That innocent-looking gadget sits there 24 hours a day, ready to connect you with any part of the world. It may be dozing, but never sleeps. It can tune you in to a success or dial you into a failure. You should realize the importance of a phone conversation. Many a business deal has been closed over the phone, and many have been lost.

FOLLOW THE EXAMPLE OF THE SWITCHBOARD OPERATOR

In business, your switchboard operator is your contact with that fast-moving, competitive, outside world. She can be more valuable than a junior executive or as detrimental as a dishonest employee.

Upon hearing this remark, a corporation president said, "Make that 5 junior executives and a vice president, and you can quote me."

A switchboard operator should be well-schooled in the following:

1. A complete understanding of her position.
2. Sufficient knowledge of the company's business, its departments, and its personnel.
3. How department heads and executives want their phone calls handled.
4. A voice that is soft, interesting, and above all, pleasant.
5. The ability to handle all types of individuals, particularly those who are unreasonable, those who do not know to whom they want to talk, and last, the downright impossible person.

I know a switchboard operator who can start your whole day off on the pleasant side by the way she says, "Good morning, Smith & Company." Her voice reeks with friendliness and understanding. She makes you feel that she has been sitting there just waiting for you to call.

I know of a switchboard operator who makes such an impression on customers and prospects that they made a special trip to the office so they can meet her and say "hello" in person.

Recently, a company which had several switchboard operators and had been receiving complaints about their attitude on the phone formulated a unique program.

First, a recording was made of a switchboard operator answering "the board," as they call it. She had a most friendly and unusual voice. This three-minute recording included everything from a mere "Hello" to handling difficult and impatient callers.

Second, each girl was called in. The importance of their position was explained to them. The recording was played, and they were asked to comment on it. Each was then told that a periodic recording would be made of her voice as she handled the switchboard.

Third, a large mirror was placed on top of the switchboard and tilted down so they could see the expression on their faces when they were answering the phone, the theory being if you do not look friendly you will not sound friendly.

Every two weeks for a period of two months they were called in. The recording of their own voices was played for them, and they were asked to comment. Then the other recording was replayed for them.

At the end of three months, the company had two excellent switchboard operators. The third asked to be transferred to the bookkeeping department, where she is happy and doing a good job.

Having started with the girl at the switchboard, let's move to that friend or enemy who sits at the executive desk.

This phone should be answered as though the person on the other end is about to inform you that you just won $5,000 in the Irish Sweepstakes, and not like the voice on the other end is about to say, "This is the Internal Revenue Service. We will be over tomorrow to check your last three years' returns."

GUARD AGAINST "TELEPHONITIS"

The phone on the executive's desk is more important today than ever. It will continue to grow more important. Time is one of the few things you cannot buy, but the proper use of the phone will let you borrow some. Conferences can be held on a phone tie-up. Important information can be gathered in a short period of time from all parts of the world. But this little gadget can also be your downfall.

One of the present day business plagues that this useful instrument causes is "Telephonitis." The symptoms are easily recognized:

1. The individual's phone is always busy.
2. He is handling or trying to handle matters that should be referred to someone else.

3. When he makes an important call, he has no idea of just exactly what he is going to say or how he is going to say it.
4. He does not know how to end a conversation that is drifting off-course.
5. He tries to handle matters by phone that should be handled by letter so that there is no possibility of misunderstanding on important items.
6. He tries to settle matters on the phone that can be settled only by a personal conference.
7. He explains an unimportant matter in great detail.

Jim McDonald ordered some new golf clubs from the Pro at the club. He wanted them for Saturday's two-ball tournament. Wednesday the Pro had guaranteed Jim the clubs would be in by Friday, and he could drop by and hit a few balls. Thursday, the Pro finds out the clubs won't be in until the following Wednesday. He puts in a call to the salesman. This is a ten-minute conversation. Then he calls the factory and talks to three different people, all of whom go into great detail about what held up the order and that they were doing everything possible, but the clubs would not be shipped before Monday. This was a 20-minute, long-distance call.

Now the Pro has to call Jim. He has the sad task of telling him that those "dream clubs" he talked him into buying won't be here Friday to hit some balls, nor on Saturday for the tournament.

Jim McDonald is a busy man. The Pro knows that,

but he calls him. He had not thought out beforehand what he would say or how he would say it. So, after "hemming and hawing" for five minutes, he finally said, "Jim, I am going to check up on those clubs of yours, and see if they are over at the express office. I'll call you back later this afternoon."

During all of this time, two people have been waiting to take a lesson at the $15 per hour rate. But the Pro had other problems. Jim is a director of the club, an important person. He is chairman of the committee that recommends whether or not the Pro's contract will be renewed next year.

So the Pro spends the next half hour calling some of his friends who are pros at nearby clubs. They have little to offer. Now there are three people, two members' wives and a member waiting to take that half-hour lesson that was scheduled an hour ago.

We won't finish the story about the Pro and Jim McDonald. You finish it. Try, if you can, to figure out what the Pro is going to tell Mr. McDonald when he calls him at 15 minutes before "going-home time," when Jim is busy trying to wind up his day's work.

Now, let's start over again where the Pro finds out the clubs he promised Jim won't be in until the following Wednesday. But now he is going to use that little gadget, the phone, as his friend.

He makes a two-minute phone call to Bob Shaw. Bob just bought a set of clubs like Jim ordered, and the Pro remembered Bob saying he was going fishing over the weekend.

Now here is the 40-second phone call the Pro made

to Jim McDonald. "Mr. McDonald, this is the Pro at the club. You remember my telling you that Mr. Shaw bought a set of clubs like the ones you ordered. Well, I just talked to him and he is going fishing over this weekend. He wants you to try his clubs if yours don't get in. Yes, I've checked. I am afraid they won't be in by Saturday, Mr. McDonald. But if you can drop by the club today or Friday I would like to take a look at you hitting some balls with those new clubs."

Every executive should be able to use the phone to his advantage, not to his or her disadvantage. One last thing, never get into an argument over the phone. Arrange a time when you can talk it over in person. Remember, if the person on the other end hangs up in the middle of an argument, you may never get an opportunity to give that fine rebuttal you so carefully thought out.

SUCCESS COMES MUCH EASIER WHEN YOU ARE PERSONABLE

When you are striving for success, you might as well have all of your good traits working for you. Being personable is one of the most important. If you will ask yourself, why do I like to have Mr. Brown wait on me at the department store, or why did I buy that insurance from Tim when I had so many friends in the insurance business; the answer probably is because both Mr. Brown and Tim are such personable individuals you have always felt that they had your interest at heart.

Being a friendly and personable individual can help you in many ways:

- People will remember you.
- People like to be with friendly, personable individuals, even though they might not be personable themselves.
- Most leaders are personable.
- Many times it will balance out some of the abilities you are lacking.
- Friendly, personable individuals not only mature more gracefully, but it seems that their faces do not seem to age as rapidly as those with a constant frown and a mouth turned down at both ends.
- Being friendly and personable can become so much a part of you, that you hardly realize why you are an INDIVIDUAL THAT YOU AND YOUR FRIENDS LIKE.

POINTS TO REMEMBER ABOUT BEING AN INDIVIDUAL THAT YOU AND YOUR FRIENDS LIKE

- You probably do not know how you appear to others; and you may very well be unaware of the effects of your actions on others.

- Try to envision yourself in different situations—sleeping, mad, telling a joke, embarrassed, being critical, tipsy, etc.

- Start a new loose-leaf notebook page and entitle it "Things I Learn About Myself." On it, make notes about the things you learn about yourself, both good and bad.

- Friendliness is the most disarming weapon that any individual can possess. Make an effort to be friendly.

- Determine what you like and what you dislike in other people; study your findings in relation to your own personality. What can you learn from these people? Can these findings help you better yourself?

- Don't let your personality get tied up by such things as the telephone—AVOID TELEPHONITIS.

- *Remember:* Success comes much easier when you are personable.

3

Don't Be Afraid to Be Different

How many times have you heard, "Now, why didn't I think of that?" The fact is, many times things are thought of, but they seem so different, so ridiculous, that they are dismissed from our minds before we give them much consideration.

I am sure if you were a young doctor 25 years ago and suggested a patient get out of bed and walk around 4 or 5 days after an appendectomy or that a person who had a heart attack might be playing golf later in the season, you not only would be considered different, but possibly a menace to the medical profession. But today, if there are no complications, 4 or 5 days after an appendectomy is considered the usual time for the patient to start his roaming around the hospital corridors.

Since the title of this chapter is, "Don't Be Afraid To Be Different," this book should have the courage to be different, in that there will not be any tests for you to take, no charts to fill out, no diagrams to study or check. The only requirement is a loose-leaf notebook to make notes plus a tape recorder. If you do not have a tape recorder, and cannot borrow one, use your imagination or your friends.

HOW TO DO SOMETHING DIFFERENT EVERY DAY

If your life is going to be interesting, if you are going to enjoy the excitement of meeting a challenge, then you must be willing to try doing things in a little different manner.

What each of us can do different each day depends upon our own individuality. What is a daily routine for one person might be something different for another. In deciding what you might do that is a little different each day, it helps to be systematic. The day can be divided into the morning, afternoon, and evening, or it can be divided into categories like work, pleasure and hobbies, and family. Drag out your imagination and try at least for one day to get out of your drab, daily routine, and do something a little different.

A LITTLE DIFFERENCE CAN MAKE THE DIFFERENCE

In every office—in every organization—there are many people who are on the same level. Each one inwardly has the feeling of wanting a little more recognition than the others in the group. Doing things just a little differently can make you stand out above the rest. Do not be satisfied with merely doing a good job. Strive for an *exceptional* job done in a little different manner.

I attended a luncheon where the speaker had a very different approach to keeping the attention of his audience of businessmen. Experience had taught him two important things: First, that time always ran out before the speaker finished at these types of luncheons, and always near the end you could see those crouching figures sneaking out. Second, that the speaker had to do something to keep the attention of these men, many of whom had to be back at the office on time.

This speaker did not wait until the end of his talk to conduct a question-and-answer period. His talk was divided into about six parts. Each part was about three minutes. At the end of each three minutes, he would say, "Now, are there any questions? I have time only for two, so make them good." He evidently had several "plants" in the audience, because there were always several questions.

He seemed to have an unlimited supply of cigars in his "handkerchief" pocket. When a good question was asked, which averaged about two out of three, he would whip out a cigar. "That question," he would half shout, "deserves a good cigar." Then, with uncanny accuracy he would throw a strike to the gentleman who had asked the question.

I watched this unusual speaker hold the attention of his audience with his cigar throwing act while he was delivering a well-organized and interesting talk.

If you have ever witnessed a photograph finish of the horses at the wire, you well realize that a little difference can make the difference.

When you have decided on doing something, pause a second before you proceed. See if you can think of something that would be just a little different from what you did before or a little different from the way it was done by the person before you. Do not be different just to be different; be practical in your thinking.

OLD IDEAS AND PROCEDURES CAN BE DRESSED UP TO LOOK DIFFERENT

One of the best-dressed office workers I have ever seen was a young 20-year-old girl who had come to Chicago from a small Illinois town. She was not only personable and immaculate, but she never seemed to wear the same outfit twice. I knew that she did not earn enough to have the wardrobe she seemed to have, but day after day she wore something not only different, but attractive.

After she left the office for a better position, I found out her secret. She started making her own clothes when she was 14 years old. When she stopped making her own clothes, she started to change the clothes she bought.

Here is what she did.

First, she bought the latest fashion magazines.

Second, she attended all sales of women's clothes, including rummage sales.

Third, she had that unique ability of visualizing what could be done with a dress hanging on a "50%-off sale" rack.

Fourth, she had a room full of brooches, strands of furs, ribbons, odd shaped buttons, and belts.

Fifth, later on I found out that the first thing she would do every evening when she got home from work was to "dismantle" the outfit she wore that day—just to be sure she would not wear the same creation the next morning. Her first task every evening was to "whip up" something new to wear for the next day. She had mastered the technique of taking something and *"making it look different."*

EVERY DIFFERENCE SHOULD HAVE A PURPOSE

It is rather ridiculous to do something different if it has no purpose. No one but a mentally unbalanced individual would decide to be different by deciding that at all intersections he would stop on the green light and go through on the red. Doing something different is only as valuable as all of the other components that go to make up the whole.

You cannot take an idea that has no value and present it in a different manner and expect that it will take on a completely new look. But you can take a good idea that has value and present it in a little different manner and receive recognition, whereas if you had presented it in the usual way it might have been passed by.

As you browse through this book, you will read about persons who dare to do things in a different manner. For some of these it was not easy, nor was it natural for them. But these individuals were able to bring out into the open some of their abilities hidden within, and by developing these talents they were able to do things in such a different manner that their ideas, their speeches, their presentations stood out from the rest.

Before you make a final decision on presenting an idea, a suggestion, a program, or making a speech, give a thought to the following:

First, do I have complete knowledge of the subject?
Second, have I considered all the pros and cons?
Third, is my timing right?
Fourth, have I considered all of the possible different ways to present my idea, program, etc.?
Fifth, in formulating my idea or program, was I conscious of trying to set up the project in a little different manner as I proceeded step by step.
Sixth, when I finished and was ready to present the idea, the program, or make that speech, did I give

one last look to see if I was a little different and still in accord with my own personality, my own individuality?

TRY TO DO SOMETHING DIFFERENT OR MEET SOMEONE WHO IS DIFFERENT EACH MONTH

I have some friends who rarely watch television, and I have others who are constant viewers. Then there are those who have a few favorite programs and ignore the rest. All of us belong to one of these three classes. In trying to do something different or read something different each month, I would also suggest that you do something a little different in reference to your T.V. habits.

For instance, if you are in the "rarely viewing class," for one month try checking the T.V. programs. Read the comments in the television guides and newspapers about what the critics have to say about various programs. Read what new programs are taking over, what kind of programs they are, who are the stars. Decide on watching at least two programs you have never watched before during the month. And if you do not want to actually watch them, at least you will be a better conversationalist when T.V. programs are discussed.

If you belong to the group that watches a few, selected programs, first follow what is suggested for those who rarely watch television; then try a few new programs each month.

Now, if you belong to that group that spends every

available moment staring at that "electric picture box," try giving up some of those programs and do a little reading. If you are not much of a reader, start with short readings on something you are interested in.

I do not think that there is anything as fascinating as meeting different people, particularly if they have something new, different, and interesting to offer. I am sure that the people who spend their vacations in different parts of the United States and sometimes visit other countries are most interesting, and you will also agree with me that meeting people who represent different views, different customs, and different hobbies is most stimulating.

I know an individual who, when he was a young lawyer, had a confirmed opinion that if he could meet ten different individuals every month, whether in the neighborhood, at church, in clubs, or on the golf course, and let these people know that he was a lawyer, he could within a few years build up a good clientele.

I do not know whether he carried out his program for meeting people or not, but I do know that in a very few years he had a very profitable law practice.

POINTS TO REMEMBER ABOUT NOT BEING AFRAID TO BE DIFFERENT

- Use your notebook to help you be different. If you have a tape recorder, that will help too.
- If your life is to be interesting, you must be willing to break old habits. Examine your

daily routine and see where you can make it different and more interesting.

- A little difference can make *the* difference. If you want more recognition than you are presently getting, dare to think differently and *be* different.

- Before acting on decisions, pause for just a second and see if you can think of a better way that's just a little different from traditional lines of thought.

- Being "different" for its own sake alone is worthless. Make sure that the "different" thing you do really makes a difference—that is, that it has purpose and is in accord with your own personality.

- Start a definite program to do something different or meet someone who is different each month.

4

Are You Standing in the Shadow of Your Best Personality?

EVERYONE HAS SEVERAL PERSONALITIES

I know a young man, a junior executive, who has an adorable wife, four lovable children, and one of the most pleasing personalities I have ever encountered. I know all of this because a year ago at Christmastime I spent four delightful hours with him and his family.

Had I not dropped by his house that day, I would have never dreamed he had such a spendid family, or that he was anything but a complaining, negative-minded, indecisive individual. He had never mentioned his wife or family in the business dealings I had with him.

There was no doubt that he was standing in the shadow of his best personality. He owed his best to the people he was associated with, to his neighbors, and his family. I do not know what he was trying to prove by using his worst personality for business. The last time I saw him he was still carrying the worries of the business world on his shoulders, supported only by the shadows of his best personality. Oh, yes, he was nursing an ulcer.

Each individual has many sides to his or her personality. There are good sides, bad sides, undeveloped sides, and unknown sides.

Select a person you like and have known for some time. Write down in your loose-leaf notebook all of the various sides of his or her personality that you have noticed and the circumstances under which they came to your attention. Now see if you feel that you have some of these personality traits. If so, underline the ones that you believe might pertain to you.

A pleasing personality, one that is developed to bring forth the best side of your own individuality, is one of the greatest assets that you can possess. It cannot be stolen or lost in the stock market, and with a little encouragement it will grow to help you when situations become difficult, when you need help, when everything else fails. It is not easy to have a pleasing personality, but it is possible.

First, if you do not have a naturally good personality, it will take a little effort on your part.

Second, you should find someone you like to use as an

example, not to copy, but to watch and see how he or she smiles and reacts. Note what he or she does under various situations.

Third, decide for a day, or a morning, or an evening that you will not complain, but give a friendly smile to everyone you speak to.

Fourth, do not be self-conscious; practice this before a mirror. See how you look when you say, "Well, hello there, it's so nice to see you." Try it again. Try to believe what you are saying this time. O.K., now let's get out the tape recorder. Try it on the recorder and see how you sound.

Work out some of your own sayings. Keep them friendly; keep your own individuality in mind. Imagine you are speaking to different people you know, ones you like—record, erase, record. Try to be a little more friendly, a little more bubbling each time.

Let's take a look at some of the good and bad inward feelings and other things that affect our personality.

Good:

Wanting to help others.

The ability to smile and occasionally to laugh right out loud.

Looking on the bright side.

A firm handshake, plus a slight twinkle of the eyes.

A pleasant and interesting voice.

Good manners.

To give and accept advice in a gracious, understanding manner.
To be available when needed.

BAD:

Constant complainer.
Envy—resentment.
Poor sport.
Inability to accept constructive criticism.
Late for appointments.
Artificial smile.
Avoiding responsibility.
Always creating the feeling that you are being taken advantage of, that you are not liked, that you are overworked, that your efforts are not appreciated, that you are the unluckiest person on earth, that you have some unknown sickness yet un-named, that you are a natural born loser, etc.

If you note a few things listed under "BAD" that pertain to you, and you can smile when you read them, you are on the right track. You have taken one step toward stepping out of the shadow of your best personality.

AN UNFRIENDLY FACE CREATES SUSPICION

Some people never forget first impressions. Do not show by your facial expression what is on your mind when you meet and are introduced to someone. What do I mean? Simply this. Many times you have heard about the person whom you are meeting for the first time. Maybe what you heard was only a rumor, but if your face reflects that you are trying to figure out or trying to decide whether you are going to like this individual, then you will usually display an unfriendly face that can only create suspicion.

When you meet people, whether you have heard about them or not, give them the best and friendliest smile you have. Think what you want, but let them see the bright side of your personality.

I have met people who for some reason or another reflected unfriendliness. Not only did the expression of their face show it, but also their movements. After I got to know some of these individuals, I found that they really were not unfriendly, but merely suspicious. Here we have the "an unfriendly face creates suspicion" in reverse—"A suspicious person creates an unfriendly face."

The unfortunate part about the individuals who reflect unfriendliness when they are not really unfriendly is that many people will not take the time, or possibly will not have the opportunity, to discover the true worth and the real personality of these unfortunate people. As a result, they miss opportunities, companionship, and understanding as they stand in the shadow of their best personality.

NEVER ARGUE OR EAT WHEN YOU ARE MAD

Very few people ever win an argument when they are mad. To begin with, they lose their composure, their reasoning gets a little warped, and they are so busy figuring out what they are going to "yell back" that they rarely hear what the other person has to say. Actually, you should not argue even when you are not mad. You should discuss or debate the issue, not argue.

Your best personality will usually hide in the deepest shadow when you are mad. Conversely, you should never, never argue with a person when *he* is mad. If you find this happening, it is always best to say, "Let's continue the discussion when we are not so excited." And if he screams "Who's excited?," try to reply calmly, "I think I am."

Improper eating habits are the cause of many ailments. I believe we can agree that a person who is ailing is seldom showing the best side of his or her personality. Eating when you are mad can have the following effects:

1. Creates an acid condition in your stomach.
2. Food is swallowed before it is chewed and has a chance to mix with the saliva of the mouth.
3. The food which is usually gulped when a person is mad allows a lot of air to filter into the stomach.

If eating when you are mad is one of your regular habits, you are on your way to giving birth to one of those nasty things called an *ulcer.* Eating should be one of the most important parts of your day. Rush, rush and eating a sandwich on the fly is not the answer to good health.

There is one thing that people from abroad very seldom understand about Americans, and that is our eating habits. They make a ceremony about dining. Eating to them is a time for relaxing and enjoyment. They select their wines and their food with great care. We use the dining period to close business deals and tell about our latest fishing trip or golf match. At home, the dinner table at times resembles the United Nations, where all family problems whether related or unrelated are argued, debated and settled, at least until the next meal.

THE SHADOWS WILL GROW DEEPER

The best side of your personality is a good deal like a muscle. If it is not used, if it lurks in the shadows when it should be exercising itself to your advantage, it will retreat deeper into the shadows until you will not be able to find it and bring it out when you need it.

Find your best personality and bring it out of the shadows.

POINTS TO REMEMBER THAT WILL HELP YOU KEEP FROM STANDING IN THE SHADOW OF YOUR BEST SELF

- Don't let yourself be like the junior executive who showed an unpleasant face to the world while having much to be thankful for.
- Write in your notebook an analysis of someone you like. List the good and the bad sides of his or her personality. Underline the ones that pertain to your personality.

- A pleasing personality is one of the greatest assets you can possess. It can be depended upon when everything else fails or is lost. Study carefully the plan for developing a pleasing personality in Chapter 4.
    - a. Developing a good personality takes effort.
    - b. Use someone you like as an example.
    - c. Decide not to complain during a specific period of time—a day, an afternoon, a morning.
    - d. Try to eliminate self-consciousness by practicing in front of a mirror or recording your voice on a tape recorder.

- Be especially concerned about the first impression you make. Remember that an unfriendly face will get you off to a bad start with most people.

- Protect your good personality and your health by refusing to argue or eat when you are mad.

5

Wake Up As an Individual

THE ART OF STARTING THE DAY RIGHT

I know a well-known doctor who upon awakening starts his day with the following short prayer:

> Thank you, Lord, for again allowing me to live through the night.

I asked him if he didn't ever ask for any help during the day. Here was his answer. "Very seldom. You see, during the day I feel it is up to me to use all of my abilities to rely upon myself and not to bother the Lord with things I can or should do myself; but at night, once asleep, I cannot consciously do anything about staying alive or waking up."

Starting the day with the proper attitude is important. This is not always easy. We may have had a restless night, not enough sleep, too much to eat or drink; or the day before may have been a "toughy," and the day ahead is waiting for us with its problems, its tensions, its disappointments. And yet, we know we must crawl out of that protective cover and start the day the best we can.

Since we are all individuals, we have our own personal problems in trying to wake up and get going. You have heard people say: "I just do not seem to wake up until about noon," or "I've got to have that cigarette and cup of coffee before I can get my eyes open."

Some individuals seem to have the knack of bouncing out of bed as though just outside the door there were a friendly world with no complications waiting for them. But for most of us, waking up and starting the day right is an ordeal. But there are certain things that each of us can do that will help us get started in the right direction.

STRETCHING AND BREATHING DEEPLY BEFORE YOU ARISE

When you awake your body is not functioning 100 per cent. You have been using only a portion of your lungs breathing during the night. Your muscles have been at rest. Stretching and breathing deeply for two minutes will fill your lungs full of fresh oxygen. Stretching will loosen up your muscles.

For those individuals who would like to wake up

quicker, spend another minute before an open window. Stretch your arms back, take a deep breath, bend over and pump your arms, crossing your arms over your abdomen as you pump. Then raise up, stretch, throw the arms back and take another deep breath. Repeat the arm pumping. After one minute of this, you should be wide awake.

Allow yourself an extra 15 minutes to dress and have a leisurely breakfast. If you are going to start your mornings fighting the clock, you will find that it is the toughest opponent you have ever met.

You should have an outline that you prepared the day before something like this:

Morning appointments—matters to be accomplished: A, B, C, etc.
Emergency matters—things that come up that must be handled immediately. When this happens you by-pass the matters set up for the morning, reschedule them for the afternoon or the next day.
Lunch data—
Afternoon—A, B, C, . . .
Matters to be handled if time permits—A, B, C,

By keeping this outline up-to-date, you start your day with a program instead of worrying about one thing while you are trying to do something else. This program has several advantages:

First, what you do not get done you can put on the agenda for the next day.

Second, all of us have things we dislike doing. After you recopy this "dislike" about four times and it keeps showing up on the next day's agenda, it starts haunting you and you take care of it.

Third, you do not forget important things that should be done and the order in which they should be taken care of.

Fourth, you make out this list the day before. This is done at the end of the day when you are clearing your desk and should know what matters you did not complete, and where you would like to enter these items on tomorrow's program.

TAKE AN HONEST LOOK AT YOURSELF AND THE DAY AHEAD

After you are sure you are awake and have had your cup of coffee or whatever you might have had, give a little thought to the day ahead.

Many successful individuals select their clothes for the day with great care. These people believe that the right attire for the day will not only give them a feeling of confidence, but will reflect the importance of the position they hold. This will, to a great extent, help them in their dealings with others.

Then, there are those individuals who have slept to the last minute, who have not the slightest idea about what they should wear, and who are better known as the "grab it and put it on" type, who often then find themselves at the office with one brown shoe and one black shoe.

Unless you are a scientist or a noted character, give some thought to your wardrobe. Here are some suggestions:

1. Give as much thought to the clothes you buy as you would to buying a new car.
2. Do not follow the latest styles if you are not the type.
3. Find out what colors suit you.
4. Learn the correct wear for all occasions.
5. Have a tailor or a clothing consultant that you have confidence in and who knows you and is acquainted with your personality.
6. Let your clothes do part of your work.

Try giving some thought before you go to bed to what you will wear the next day. You can always change your mind the next morning. When you leave for work, be the best dressed individual that you can be.

TRY TO THINK OF SOMETHING PLEASANT FOR THE DAY AHEAD

Every day will contain both pleasant and unpleasant events. Some of these we know beforehand; others sneak up on us before we are ready. It is just as easy to start the day by thinking of the pleasant things, and handle the unpleasant matters as they come along.

Do not get yourself involved emotionally before the day begins. Try to think of something pleasant when you are shaving or when putting on your makeup, depending upon your gender.

See if that face in the mirror reflects an interesting, pleasant day ahead. If it doesn't, give it a chance. Make an effort to smile and think of something pleasant. Remember that important person, you, deserves a good start for that involved day ahead.

DON'T FRET ABOUT THINGS THAT YOU CANNOT DO ANYTHING ABOUT

Fretting about things you cannot do anything about creates more frustration than any other single factor. I believe that it can be a forerunner and a contributor to ulcers, high blood pressure, and similar disorders.

Here are some suggestions to handle things that you cannot do anything about. If some of these suggestions seem slightly out in left field, remember fretting about most of these matters is crazy in the first place.

a. Quit thinking about them, and they will go away.
b. Write them in next year's diary.
c. Only think about these disturbing matters when you are taking a steam bath.
d. Reduce them to writing and then throw them in a waste basket labeled "Filing cabinet for things I cannot do anything about."
e. Set up a special book for recording these matters. Label this book "Do not open until Christmas." Open and burn every Christmas Eve.

If you try to reason with things you cannot do anything about, you are lost. Save your energy and your sanity by doing something on those matters that have an answer.

POINTS TO REMEMBER ABOUT WAKING UP AS AN INDIVIDUAL AND STARTING THE DAY RIGHT

- The most important part of your day is very probably the few moments when you are waking up. These few seconds can condition the way you think and feel for the rest of the day.
- Use the suggested stretching and breathing exercises to wake up your body 100 per cent. Allow yourself plenty of time for dressing and for breakfast, don't let yourself be rushed.
- Outline your day in advance. Follow the suggested format in this chapter; it will help you get more done with less stress and strain. Remember—this outline should be prepared the day before it is to be used.
- Give great attention to the matter of your daily dress. The overused expression, "clothes make the man," has a great deal of truth in it, as many top executives well know.
- Try to anticipate pleasant things in the day ahead. At the same time de-emphasize—in your mind—the negative things that you may have to face.

6

Flexible Individuals Usually Succeed

EVERYONE HAS FLEXIBLE CHARACTERISTICS

One of the most flexible persons I ever met was a labor relations attorney. He was not only flexible, but successful. I have seen him barge into a conference room with confidence and determination written all over his face. He practically ripped open his brief case; and after checking paper after paper, he said very firmly: "I'm sorry, but I forgot an important document. I'll be back in fifteen minutes."

Before anyone could say a word, he was gone. Then they waited for him to barge back into the room. Twenty minutes later he appeared at the door smoking a big cigar—a self satisfied grin had replaced that disturbed look. Slowly, he walked over to the conference table and sat down. He did not bother to open his brief case or produce the supposed document that seemed so important fifteen minutes before.

I asked John what he had in mind with the barging in and out routine, and then showing up with nothing but a silly grin and a big cigar. He just laughed, and said:

"I really didn't have anything in mind; that was my problem. I needed a little more time before disclosing my hand. To ask for time would have, well, disclosed my hand, showing that I had nothing in mind. This I could not afford. So, if you will remember what happened when I returned, all we did was spar around for a few hours, then continued the meeting for a week. That week was all I needed to gather a few facts and a little understanding that resulted in a workable contract for both sides."

John then added one last remark that I especially remember, "When things are tough, when the going is real tough, don't let the other side figure you out. If you are hard to figure out, you are real difficult to *OUTFIGURE*."

CHECK YOUR OWN FLEXIBILITY

Flexibility is a great asset. It ranks along with personality, know-how, enthusiasm, courage and determination. Everyone has flexible traits. Some of us do not use these traits. We want to act the way we feel, rather than the way that would benefit us the most. Let's ask ourselves a few questions about our own flexibility:

Can you be calm when the other fellow is blowing his top?
Can you compliment a person you do not particularly like?
Can you be at ease when unexpected people drop in on you?
Can you laugh at a joke you have heard before?
Can you give a short talk when called upon unexpectedly?
Can you change a planned routine when the unexpected happens without being disturbed?
Can you act at ease in new surroundings with new people?
Do you know when to speak and when to listen?
Do you have the ability to express yourself on a controversial subject without incurring animosity?

If you can do 75 per cent of these things, you are quite a flexible person.

CAN YOU BE AT EASE AND STILL BE FLEXIBLE?

The above statement may seem paradoxical, but it is very true. How this can be done is not as difficult as it might appear.

First, develop your own flexibility.
Second, always be aware of:
a. The occasion.

b. People present.
c. The impression you wish to leave.
d. The various sides of your own personality, and how and when to use each side by being able to be a good listener, a well-informed person, an individual with a good sense of humor and a personable and interesting disposition.

You will find that by knowing your own capabilities, and how and when to bring them into play, you will feel at ease while you are being flexible.

PEOPLE WHO FIT INTO ANY SITUATION ARE THE MOST SUCCESSFUL

I think the above statement explains itself. Very seldom are we able to set up a situation as we would like it. Often the situation changes before we are quite sure what the situation is. The ability to fit in with the changing situation is not only one of the ingredients of success, but many times you change the situation to your liking and benefit.

FORMULATE A FLEXIBLE PERSONALITY OF YOUR OWN

Here again, you should follow some of the suggestions made in other chapters by first taking an honest look at yourself; and, second, studying others whom you have seen being flexible with the greatest of ease.

Go back to page 64 in this chapter and make a list

of the questions you answered "No." See what you can do to make these answers "Yes." This should help you formulate a flexible personality of your own.

POINTS TO REMEMBER ABOUT KEEPING YOUR PERSONALITY FLEXIBLE

- Flexibility is a great asset in meeting the ever-changing circumstances of daily life. Check yourself to see how your flexible characteristics measure up.
- The ideal to strive for is that of remaining at ease while maintaining maximum flexibility. This involves a knowledge of your own capabilities and how and when to bring them into play.
- It is self-evident that the most successful people are generally the most flexible. Of course, it is not the only requirement for success, but it is a very substantial ingredient.
- The trait of flexibility also fits in with our concept of developing a pleasing personality. The most pleasing people we know can generally fit into almost any situation—they are flexible.

7

Individuals Who Keep On Trying Never Fail

Within our own capacity, the ability and courage to keep trying is the guide to ultimate success. Many individuals become great by overcoming handicaps. Glen Cunningham, the great miler, started running to get circulation in his legs after they were badly burned. The desire to keep trying, plus the courage to start over and over again, is the formula that lies behind the success of many ordinary individuals.

WISHFUL THINKING IS NOT ENOUGH

Wishful thinking is best illustrated by New Year's resolutions.

All of us have at one time or another made resolutions that were on the wishful side. Some of us make the same resolutions each year. We have been doing it for decades.

The trouble with New Year's resolutions is:

They are made half-heartedly.

Very seldom are these resolutions reduced to writing.

No program is formulated to carry out the resolutions.

Little consideration is given to why these resolutions fell by the way-side the year before.

We seldom take them seriously; and, oh yes, we can start all over again next year.

The story of a friend and client of mine named Fred illustrates better than any lessons, instructions or lectures what an individual can accomplish who keeps on trying.

Fred was born in Sweden. He came to this country at the turn of the century. He didn't speak English and had very little money. He came to the Middle West because that is where a few of his friends from Sweden had settled five years ago.

After spending a day in New York and seeing the city mushrooming on all sides, Fred had the feeling that someday he would be a big builder. But thinking that someday you will be a big contractor, when you have no money, no connections, do not know a trade, and your English is limited to about 20 words, is bordering on the "Wishful Thinking" side.

But Fred was more than a wishful thinker. He had a very simple plan. First, he had to get a job, any kind of a job, so he could eat. The only thing Fred could find was a job as a laborer on a railroad section gang.

He made only one request when he was being assigned to a gang:

"Please, no put me wit Swedes, I no learn to speak English wit them."

Fred did not move very fast the first year. Although he now spoke good, broken English, he was a long way away from the construction business.

It was during his third year when Fred coined his famous four- and five-word questions that were the basis of his success. He continually kept asking these two questions: "How much you make?" and when he found out that a person made more than he did, he would ask, "How you get that job?"

When Fred found out that bricklayers made almost twice as much as he did, he asked every bricklayer he met, "How you get that job?" Fred was a good bricklayer. He watched other tradesmen and during lunchtime he would ask a lot of questions. He learned to read blueprints. Then one day while he was working on a repair job in a factory, the boiler blew up and Fred found himself in a four bed ward in a hospital.

In the bed next to Fred was a carpenter. He was a very friendly, talkative Irishman. It didn't take long for Fred to find out that carpenters made more than bricklayers. "How you get that job?" he asked.

Well, the Irishman's brother-in-law was one of the "big-wigs" in the carpenters' union. He also had some good connections with some builders. By the time Fred was released from the hospital, he had shaken hands with the Irishman at least 20 times to bind the promise that he would get Fred into the carpenters' union.

Fred's start as a carpenter was far from sensational. If it had not been for his friend, the Irishman, he would have been back with the bricklayers. But with his often cut and bandaged fingers, Fred improved. He continued to learn about the other trades and always asked the question, "How much you make?"

Then one day during the lunch hour, his friend the Irishman stopped by. He was all dressed-up and smoking a big cigar.

"How come you all dressed-up and no work?" Fred asked.

The Irishman flicked a few ashes off the end of his cigar, and with a slight wave of his hand and an air of importance, said; "I'm a builder now."

"A builder. How you get to be builder?"

When Fred found out that his friend had bought three lots, then got some plans and a banker to finance him, and had put up the three lots for security while he completed a house on the first lot, he put all of his savings in real estate. A few years later, he was building houses, then small apartments, schools, factories, etc.

Before the depression of the thirties hit, Fred was a millionaire. But like a lot of people, Fred tried holding on to everything he had worked so hard to get. He couldn't seem to bring himself around to forfeiting one investment to save another. When the depression had run its course, Fred had to start over again.

Fred retired a few years ago to Florida. He had made a come-back, and at the age of 80 decided to take it a little easier. But the latest report on my friend and former client is that he is building duplex apartments in Coral Gables. He must have asked someone, "How much you make building duplex apartments?"

Although Fred's success was partly due to hard work and determination, we should note the following:

He had an idea and never lost sight of his goal.
He moved ahead only one step at a time.
He was not merely a wishful thinker.
He never quit trying.
He allowed everyone to help him.
He wasn't afraid to start over.
He took each hurdle, each setback, one at a time.
He always tried to find out how the individual who was one step in front of him got there.
He had a simple formula and never got lost in unrelated details.
He was willing to stop after each advance and wait for the next step to develop.

PEOPLE WHO KEEP TRYING GENERALLY GET THE BREAKS

Some people do seem to be luckier than others, but with these lucky people I have noted the following:

1. They have a positive attitude.
2. You find very few complainers.

3. They do not sit around feeling unlucky.
4. If they get a bad break, they consider it unusual. They also feel that on account of the bad break, the next good or lucky break will be bigger than usual.

ENTHUSIASM IS NECESSARY TO KEEP TRYING

It is not always easy to start over again, to keep trying. But enthusiasm is the one thing that will give you the necessary impetus to try and try again.

DO NOT LISTEN TO THE DIEHARDS

You will never create any enthusiasm by listening to those whose by-words are:

It will never work.
It is not worth the effort.
It's been tried before.
You are not the type.
Why don't you give up?
Go to bed and forget it.
Why louse up your day by trying again?
What's the matter with you—you a nut or something?

Every venture has one or more of these "diehards." Somehow, these negative thinkers inspire me. I want to show them that if they needle me enough my desire to start over again flames into real enthusiasm. I hope that you can use some of this reverse psychology to help you when those it-can't-be-done individuals attempt to discourage you from starting over again on a venture you have faith in.

BYPASS YOUR FAILURE ON THE NEXT TRY

Keep a record of your failures as well as your successes. Before you start over again, check these failures. Set up a program on how to by-pass them on the next try. Do not start over until you have figured a reason for these failures, and decided on a method of overcoming them when you try again with a new program.

POINTS TO REMEMBER ABOUT HOW TO KEEP ON TRYING

- Persistent, steady effort—the desire and the ability to keep on trying—is the ultimate key to success.
- Wishful thinking is not enough to ensure success. Real effort on the action level must accompany mental inspiration.
- What is often called "luck," is more often than not a combination of very real, dynamic personality traits. Remember the example of Fred the Swede; he "made his own luck."
- You must develop a sense of enthusiasm to get your dreams transformed into realities. Don't listen to the scoffers. The ever-sceptical attitude prevents positive steps toward success.

8

How to Beat the Pressure of the Fast Tempo of Modern Times

If I were reading this book instead of writing it and read the above title, I would immediately think, What am I going to read here that I haven't read before? How many don'ts are listed? How many questions will I have to answer so I can be classified, analyzed, and pinned up for inspection?

The fact it, there aren't any questions. Any questions that are to be answered will have to come from within *you*. You as an individual will have to make your own decisions and formulate your own program. What is work for one individual can be a hobby for another. What causes anxiety and frustration in one person might have no effect on his neighbor or the fellow in the next office. Each individual must determine for himself the things that disturb, irritate, and bother him and then formulate his own program to beat the tension and pressure of modern times.

One of the best ways to start a program is to study and watch other people who seem to have acquired the knack of operating under stress or strain with little or no effort. The fact is there are certain individuals who enjoy the daily rat-race where the rats grow bigger and the pace gets faster. To them, it is a challenge, like making a hole in one or picking horses in the daily double.

Take politics—I do not believe that there is a more frustrating, nerve-wracking, disappointing, ulcer-inviting, and time-consuming way of life. But, in spite of all of this, look at the ages of some of our Twentieth Century politicians. Herbert Hoover wrote six books after he was 80 years old. Former Vice President "Cactus Jack" Garner was still alive on his 95th birthday. President Truman outwalked the reporters when he was 75 years of age. And the former Chief Justice Oliver Wendell Holmes, upon seeing a beautiful girl, said, "I wish I were 70 again." He was 94 at the time.

I do not know the secret or the formula of these gentlemen, but I do know the story of a politician who figured out for himself a very unique program of survival. He knew that one big problem all politicians encountered was banquets. Banquets meant eating and drinking. Eating and drinking meant overweight. Overweight could lead to almost anything. So, before every banquet or cocktail party, he decided beforehand what and how much he would drink and eat. He had the ability to nurse a scotch and soda, with ice added at various intervals, for an hour or more. For those well-wishers who loved to drink, he was always with a drink in hand. When the time came to hit the campaign trail, where night after night he was required to speak at from 8 to 10 different political meetings, he became an unusual individual who finished the evening as fresh as when he started. His program was simple for him because it was his own. Here it is.

If he had 10 ward meetings to make, he got out his personal record cards of these wards. These cards were kept up-to-date by his secretary, containing names and personal items about the ward and its leaders. John then prepared his speech, a basic talk that could be used at all meetings. With his chauffeur, he would start his evening tour. After his first talk, he would return to the car, climb in the back seat, take off his hat and loosen his tie, lean back and take his first car nap. His chauffeur would stop the car about two blocks from the next stop. John would freshen up with his favorite lotion, relocate his tie, and study his personal card for this meeting. Sometimes when he returned to the car, he would make a note on the card of something he noticed or heard pertaining to that ward. If he had a particularly rough evening, the next day's agenda had a number of musts—number one, steam bath; number two, massage.

When the campaign was over, John was one of the

few politicians who did not have to go away on a vacation for a rest. He had been resting all through the campaign.

DON'T LET UNIMPORTANT THINGS "BUG" YOU

We generally do something about big, important things that "bug" us. But we tend to allow the little ones to irritate us over and over again. A businessman once said to me, "Tell me how I can handle the little things that bug me." I looked at him, and not knowing what bugged him, couldn't give him an answer. Finally, I said, "Listen, my friend, I am quite busy telling myself how to handle the little, unimportant things that bug *me*." Then he began to laugh. I didn't think I had said anything very funny, but evidently he did. "You know," he said, "you just hit the nail right on the head. The number-one thing that bugs me the most is anybody trying to tell me what bugs me the most. It's my wife, my secretary, my doctor, my brother-in-law. Everybody seems to be in the act but me."

Now, we all allow unimportant things to bug us at times, but when we continually allow the same thing, the same person, to irritate and disturb us, we should formulate a program for handling these tensions. Before we can determine what we are going to do about the little things that bug us, let's first find out what they are, because many of us do not realize that we have them.

If you have set up a loose-leaf notebook, start another page entitled "Me and the Little Things That Bug Me." See how many things you can list and grade yourself A, B, and C—A for bigger tensions, B for medium, and C for minor ones.

Several years ago, I was a guest speaker along with Dr. William Menninger, who has done so much in developing a treatment for shell-shocked soldiers. The occasion was a young presidents' organization conference. Dr. Menninger, who heads the Menninger Hospital at Topeka, Kansas, spoke on the subject of being mentally equipped and fit to be an executive. "Everyone has a breaking point," he pointed out. "If yours is way down the ladder, you should not be an executive. If you want to fire an employee and the same day want to raise his salary, you should not be an executive."

Dr. Menninger reviewed accident reports of employees who had accidents on the way to work and accidents in the plants in the morning, and the surprising thing about the statistics was that a great percentage of accidents, both in the plant and on the way to work, happened to employees who had had a fight, an argument, or a misunderstanding with their wives before leaving home.

In the question-and-answer period that followed, one of the young presidents asked, "I would like to know, how do you keep from having an argument or misunderstanding with your wife in the morning."

A hand in the second row went up very quickly. "Would you like to answer that question?" Dr. Menninger asked.

"Yes, sir, I would. My wife and I haven't had a misunderstanding, a fight, or even an argument for over five years."

"And what is your secret?" Dr. Menninger inquired.

"Very simple—she doesn't get up in the morning."

OPERATE UNDER A PROGRAM, NOT A SCHEDULE

Buses, trains, and airplanes run on schedules. Individuals should operate on a program. Take a quick look at the following:

1. Make a list of the things that irritate you.
2. Make a list of the people who irritate you and why you think they have this effect on you.
3. Make a list of the things you despise doing and figure out why.
4. Take a look at your behavior-pattern:
   a. Do you lose your temper easily?
   b. Do you talk fast and loud when you are excited?
   c. Do you continue to work after hours or on weekends when you are tired?
   d. Do you eat and drink too much?

Here we stop, and start to formulate a program. You should have a program for yourself, one you believe in and want to follow. Check to see if you are still running when you should be walking, walking when you should be sitting, and sitting when you should be lying down. If you have slowed down to your normal pace, you are ready to proceed with your program on how to beat the pressure of modern times.

I am a firm believer that every individual should formulate his own program to beat this fast tempo we are traveling in, the reason being that if you have made an honest study of yourself, you are in the best position to know what you can do and how it can be accomplished.

In a program that is figured out for you, the usual message is in the form of a pointing finger that means, in effect, "you better do this or else." The front-runners in this fast tempo of the present time revolt at the slowed-down program that is forced upon them. They are more apt to follow their own programs and start over again when they stray. However, people tend to abandon the entire program prepared by someone else when they find it difficult to follow. If you are making notes as you browse through this book, you should be able to formulate your own program when you finish.

WHEN THINGS ARE DIFFICULT, BRING OUT YOUR HUMOR

Humor is the greatest antibiotic ever discovered. It can release tension, stop frustration, settle your nerves, make friends, dispel fear, keep you thinking young, close sales, stop arguments, and make you personable. Humor is very much like the telephone. It can be your friend or enemy. Some people confuse humor with being funny, and we are all aware of the bore who tries so hard but is just not funny.

Everyone has a sense of humor. In some, it is one of their hidden traits. They never get it out working for them.

To be effective, humor must be natural. I have seen humor disarm an antagonistic person as though he had been struck by lightning. One of the odd things about humor is that it is one of the most valuable assets a person can possess. And, it is rare to find anyone trying to develop a better sense of humor.

I have often thought that someday I might pick up a newspaper and find an ad that reads something like this:

> One of the ingredients of success is a personalized sense of humor. We are offering a six-week humor course that includes the following: Determining your type of humor; finding the full capacity and range of your humor; developing your sense of humor to its fullest extent; when, where, and how to use it; when, where and how not to use it. The last week of this course will be devoted to determining the types of jokes, if any, you should tell at parties, church gatherings, in locker rooms, and also the type you should not attempt to tell at all. The jokes selected for you will be first told by a person with your type of personality. Then you will be required to put the same jokes on tape. Your timing and tone qualities will be noted. You will then re-tape the same jokes. When you graduate, you will receive a copy of all your taped jokes for your comparison. You can add new jokes to your repertoire by putting them on tape as you hear them.

The above is not as crazy as it might seem. And it surely makes more sense than some of the ads that read "Buy this book, and you can succeed in any of the ventures listed in Chapter IV. Learn the four magic phrases that will solve any problem," or the book that says, "How to make people love you who have hated you all of their lives."

GET RID OF THE DETAILS THAT DRAG YOU DOWN

Determination is a fine characteristic, but it can be carried too far. If you find that you are fighting things just to get them done when these matters should be detailed to others under your supervision, you are doing yourself an injustice. If you are handling small details that are dragging you down and keeping you from doing important work, get rid of them. Just because something has to be done doesn't mean that you are the one who has to do it.

DEVELOP A POSITIVE MENTAL ATTITUDE

I am sure we have all heard the above many times, but have we done anything about it? I have a friend who realizes he has a tendency to think negatively. When he finds himself unconsciously doing this, he does what he calls "reverse thinking." He turns the thought around.

Here are some ideas that will help you develop a positive attitude.

First, determine what your usual attitude is.

Second, be your own analyst. What makes you think positively about certain things at certain times and negatively at others.

Third, make a note every time you find yourself thinking like this. Study these notes.

Fourth, when you can, associate with positive thinkers.

Fifth, when you are working on a project, visualize how a person with a positive attitude would approach the project.

Sixth, start each day with trying to have a positive attitude on some one thing that you know will confront you within the next 24 hours.

Seventh, formulate a program of your own. Be aware of the advantages of being a positive thinker and work slowly but definitely toward developing a positive attitude. Remember, a negative attitude creates fear and tension, all of which adds up to frustration.

POINTS TO REMEMBER ABOUT BEATING THE PRESSURE OF THE FAST TEMPO OF TODAY

- Questions about the suitability of your way of life must come from within *you.* No self-proclaimed seer can determine what pace of living is best suited to your temperament.

- Once again, turn to our method of studying the way of life of someone who seems to have succeeded in this aspect of living. Observe the tricks used by an acquaintance who seems to have mastered the knack of operating under the stresses and strains of modern times.

- Don't get tied up with details that are time-consuming and bothersome, but actually unimportant in terms of larger goals.
- Formulate your own program, using the broad principles outlined in this chapter, to beat the pressures of these times.
- Use your sense of humor as a weapon against tensions and aggravations. Keep it natural and keep it fun.
- Follow the seven steps to a positive mental attitude. Try some of the "reverse-thinking" techniques that turn negative attitudes into positive ones.

9

Husbands and Wives Can Be Happy Individuals

You have often heard, "They should never have married. They are so different." The fact is, many happily married people are direct opposites, yet they respect each other's individuality.

I have some friends who recently celebrated their 25th wedding anniversary. She told me how she happened to marry Dave. "I was going with three different boy friends at the time," she said. "All three wanted to marry me. I was only 21, and it was not easy to decide among the three. Then one night I visualized living with each of the three. When I got to the point of picking up after them, their socks and shorts in the bathroom, newspapers strewn about the floor, ashes that missed the ashtray, I knew that doing this for two of them would irk me no end, but I wouldn't mind doing it for Dave."

When you consider that a husband and wife live in such close proximity, it should not be difficult to understand that even in the best-matched and suited marriages there are misunderstandings, arguments, and pouting on both sides. So, we can well imagine what happens when the husband and wife are not completely suited for each other. But, regardless of whether they are suited or not at the time of marriage, many couples not only survive but learn to enjoy the unity that looked so beautiful when they said "I do." One of the strange things that happens in marriage is the ability of some people to adjust their differences, mature gracefully, and still retain their individuality.

On a recent trip to Florida, I stopped at St. Petersburg to visit a friend of mine who had retired a few years before. On account of his health, as well as his wife's, they were both confined to the house a good deal of the time. I was quite surprised when he went into the kitchen to get my wife and me a glass of orange juice that we could hear her yell, "See how much you can spill or break this time." When he returned with the tray and three glasses of juice, he had brought his wife's in a tin cup. As he handed it to her, he turned to me and said, "She has already broken one more dish than me this month, so until I catch up she drinks out of the tin cup." I felt very ill-at-ease because of some of the remarks that flew back and forth during our stay.

When we left, he walked out to the car with us. He must have sensed that I was a little surprised at the remarks they made to each other. "Before you leave," he said, "I want to explain something to you. Those remarks that my wife and I make to each other, well, they are sort of a game we play. You see, at our age and not having any real hobbies, we realize our minds don't get much exercise, so we kind of keep the mind active by barbing each other every chance we get. It keeps us on our toes, thinking of how to get back at the other one after a really sarcastic remark. We really get a big kick out of visits like yours today, watching the expressions on your faces, especially when my wife made the remark, "Norm has a new suit. If we knew you were coming and he would have promised not to sit down and wrinkle it or spill something on the coat or trousers, he could have worn it."

All I could say was, "I am sure glad that was all play. I wondered what happened to that good sense of humor you had up north. I was afraid for a minute that you had left it up there." We both laughed.

Later on, he wrote me that they had bought a tape recorder, and when they got going real good they put their conversation on tape. Maybe some day I will write a radio script about a retired husband and wife and their "sassy" conversation.

LEARN TO APPRECIATE AND RESPECT EACH OTHER'S INDIVIDUAL TRAITS

The first step toward a happy marriage and a successful one is to recognize that each is an individual and that both have their idiosyncrasies, their likes and their dislikes.

I once heard Dr. Preston Bradley of Chicago explain the difference between talent and genius. "Talent" he said, "is when you can with great authority and with convincing ability tell someone off. You may have been absolutely correct. Once you have exploded your profound speech you are a deflated balloon. The other person knows exactly how you feel, and you know little or nothing about how he feels. Take the husband who rightfully and with great oratory tells the little wife she has without just reason or cause gone over the budget for the third straight week. Throughout his entire speech he has shown great talent. When he has finished, she looks up at him, wets her lower lip and a tear rolls down her cheek, and in a choked voice she mutters, 'John, I don't think you love me anymore.' That's genius."

First, a husband and wife must recognize each other's individual traits. It is difficult to appreciate and respect something that you do not recognize.

Second, make a list of the other's traits and talents, then take a good look at them.

Third, study other individuals who have the same traits and talents.

Fourth, discuss without emotion how each of you can help the other person understand your feelings, your traits, and your talents. Remember that no matter how you may differ, as long as you want to be something for the other person, your marriage has a sound base and with a little effort and understanding it can become workable.

Fifth, consideration for the other person's feelings is always necessary.

Sixth, if you cannot resolve your differences, do not allow them to reach insurmountable heights. Ask for help. Go to your parish priest, minister, your rabbi, or a marriage counselor.

FIND A HOBBY THAT YOU CAN BOTH ENJOY

Finding a hobby that you both can enjoy is not as easy as it sounds. Hobbies are something that are very individual. A husband should not expect his wife, or the wife her husband, to start right off enjoying a hobby they know nothing about. When you expect a person to adopt a hobby and be simply wild about it the first time out, you are all set for a great disappointment. Let's take a couple of examples.

John Brown was an ardent fisherman, bowler, and golfer. His wife liked the arts, the theater, and bridge. We'll start with John. If he thinks he is going to make a fisherman out of Sue by taking her up into Canada to rough it, fish from morning to sunset and then stretch out for the night in his sleeping bag, he is out of his "cotton-picking" mind. However, if he could have started by going fishing with another couple, whom they both knew well, who liked to fish, who also liked nice accommodations, swimming, a little night life, and playing bridge, this new hobby might have had a chance. This first trip should only be for a long weekend.

The first tip in trying to interest anyone in a hobby is to give him an opportunity to see other people enjoying the hobby and to explain the hobby with all its working parts. Someone besides the husband or the wife should explain all about it. Then they should be fed a small portion at a time. A wife who does not understand anything about football would not enjoy sitting out in the cold with her husband, who keeps jumping up and down yelling crazy things like, hit him low; penalize him, loafer—don't kick; watch it, it's a pass. It is important to respect each other's hobbies. If you do not want to join in, at least make an attempt to understand it.

HELP THE OTHER PERSON TO DEVELOP HIS ABILITY AND TALENTS

Remember, you are a team. Don't envy the ability of your partner. Be proud of what your partner can accomplish. I remember the look on Don Carter's face when his wife won the Women's Bowling Championship in Dallas, January 1964. The great Don Carter did not finish in contention in the Men's Division, but by the smile on his face you would have thought he had won the Bowler of the Year title.

REMEMBER THAT THE OTHER PERSON IS AN INDIVIDUAL, UNLIKE ANY OTHER PERSON IN THE WORLD

If you will keep the above in mind, it will help you understand some of the things you don't understand about certain individuals. If you bring out your humor and laugh at some of the things you want to scream about, it will go a long way in relieving some of the pressure that at times builds up in the best marriages. Compliment your marriage partner every day, no matter how small or unimportant the compliment might be.

A compliment takes only a second, all it costs is a smile supported by a reassuring face. A suggestion for husbands: The next time you take the little wife out for the evening, try to visualize her as a person who is about to bequeath you one-hundred thousand dollars. And the wife: think of your husband, this evening out, as a movie celebrity who is taking you out on the town. You will be surprised at what a wonderful time the two of you will have.

POINTS TO REMEMBER ABOUT HOW TO BE A HAPPY, MARRIED INDIVIDUAL

- Even though your personality is virtually the opposite of that of your spouse, you still can achieve marital happiness. To achieve happiness under such circumstances, you must *respect each other's personality.*

- Do not stop at mere respect, however; you must actually learn to appreciate your spouse's individual traits. This demands a conscious, determined effort to recognize these traits.

- Although hobbies are very individual, try to find one that you both can enjoy. Do not force a new hobby on an uninterested husband or wife, but try to develop his or her interest by means of the methods outlined in this chapter.

- Try to help your marriage partner develop his or her talents. Don't be envious of your spouse's talents—be proud of them.

- A compliment is a small thing, but it means a a great deal to the recipient. Try to compliment your spouse at least once a day.

10

It Is Easier to Succeed Than to Fail

The first time I wrote the above slogan, I had mixed feelings. I had seen many more successes than failures. But wasn't it easier to fail? Didn't it take less effort to fail than to succeed?

Before I convinced myself that it was easier to succeed, I analyzed the slogan from all angles. I started with the natural instincts and impulses of men. I could find nothing that indicated that anyone had any built-in desire to fail—that everyone from the age of reason wanted to succeed.

The "Little Leaguer" wants to make the team. He wants a good batting average, and a good fielding record. The high school student does not enroll to flunk out or to go out for the football team and not make the squad.

So my first answer to my question was, *It is not natural to want to fail*—that within all of us is the inborn feeling and desire to succeed, and that it should be easier to do something you want to do than something you would like to avoid.

I then studied the motivating forces behind success. I found that no matter how small or how large the project, the enterprise, or the ultimate goal, there was a satisfying feeling of accomplishment; and this feeling led to enthusiasm for other projects. It gave the individuals that were a part of, or contributed to, the enterprise a feeling of well-being, of being needed, of contentment, of happiness, of moving forward, of being an individual.

I then realized that I never heard of an individual or a group of individuals organizing a program for the purpose of failing. People will devote their time, their energy, their talent to a project where the ultimate purpose is a successful venture. But you cannot entice an individual to join a cause that is aimed in a negative direction, at a guaranteed failure.

SUCCESSES BUILT ON FAILURES ARE THE BEST

If you have ever seen movies of man's first attempt to fly, you should be happy that those first attempts were failures. There were round "Venetian-blind contraptions" that bounced up and down. There were massive wings strapped to the person, and bicycle pedals that tried to flap awkward wings like a bird. But after many failures, the first successful flight was the Wright Brothers' propeller plane.

From this humble start the present day jet emerged. But there were many failures and trials and errors before it became a commercial success.

The real reason that successes built on failures are more successful is that those pitfalls can be avoided in the future. And only by eliminating the errors, the detours, do you provide a sound basis for lasting success, rather than a quick flash that disappears with the first real obstacle that comes along.

Many businesses fail because of the inability of those in charge to recognize past failures, and by not formulating a program to bypass pitfalls that others have encountered in the same field.

Here is a list of the reasons why many businesses fail; some of these are listed later on as common mistakes. These mistakes were collected from many sources, including bankruptcies, assignments for creditors, or businesses who sold out at a loss or merely closed shop.

1. Relying on one product or one customer.
2. Locating in a poor labor market or too far away from a good selling market.
3. Under-capitalized or under-financed.
4. Poor packaging and advertizing.
5. Inability to diversify products.

6. Understanding or not understanding the competition in this field.
7. Poor labor relations.
8. Wanting to do business the old way.
9. Unable to cut costs in a competitive market.
10. Top personnel going to other companies because of better company benefits, including pensions, stock options, major medical, etc.
11. Nepotism—allowing relatives who are not qualified to hold top positions and draw large salaries. (*Note:* In a survey that was made of family-owned companies that had gone bankrupt, it was found that the greater percentage failed during the reign of the third generation.)

In the case of mistake No. 11, the owners of the first generation were the pioneers. They were individuals with courage, determination, and ability. The business world was not crowded with competition and with giant corporations such as we find today.

This is the grandfather who passed on to his son money, prestige, and a successful business. The son now has money. He walks into a business without the experience or the desire, the challenge and the determination of his father who thought of the business as "his baby." He has not experienced the trials and failures that the business was built on. But the business, on account of its name and reputation, continues to be successful.

The son also inherits some "old timers" who are not in accord with the new ways of doing business. To get rid of them would of course be an insult to his father's memory. However, the business, although not as successful as under his father, is still running at a profit.

Now comes the third generation. The grandson has money, an easy way of life, and does not feel the challenge of running a successful business as did his grandfather.

He also comes into a more complicated world, with automation, keen competition, and changing methods of operation. And there is always that family tradition: keep the family company name that has been so successful in the past.

Remember, we are talking about family-controlled companies that fail, not those that succeed.

It is not uncommon for a grandfather to start a business in a small way, the son carries on and modestly increases its operation, and then along comes the grandson, a dynamic individual with ideas, courage, and foresight, and builds it into a giant.

There is a story about two sons who each inherited a business from their father. The factories and offices were located in two different cities. However, both were the same in size and produced the same products.

Fifteen years later, the number-one son went bankrupt. He had worked hard and diligently, but somehow his business, from the day he took over, had started a downward trend. When it folded, the company was still manufacturing the best buttonhooks, spats, garters, and suspenders in the country.

The number-two son, however, was most successful. By now, he had a small plant in Japan that manufactured transistor radios, wrist watches, and Christmas ornaments. His plant in Puerto Rico was producing girdles, bras, aprons, etc. The plant in the United States had gone into plastics. It was manufacturing golf bags, seat cushions, lamps, and baby furniture.

NO ONE EVER WROTE A BOOK ON THE EASY WAY TO GO BANKRUPT

If you have ever browsed around in a large bookstore, you found all kinds of books on how to succeed, how to win friends, how to do about everything except how to fail where others succeed, or how to go bankrupt your first year in business.

So one of the reasons it is easier to succeed than to fail is that everyone wants to tell you about how he succeeded and nobody wants to admit why he failed. You can take a course, read articles, get advice on most anything except "How to Go Broke Quick," "How to Invest and Lose Money," or "Be Sure to Let Your Employees Help You Fail."

HOW TO SUCCEED WHERE OTHERS HAVE FAILED

There are many reasons why certain individuals fail as well as why certain businesses fail. The first thing for you to do if you are going into a venture is to find out the reason why others failed. Then, see if you can bypass these failures.

There are many companies throughout the United States which specialize in buying up defunct companies or businesses that are about to fall apart. These companies can spot the weakness in a company's operation. It may be that the company needed capital it could not borrow or was hampered by bad management, an inadequate sales program, outmoded ways of doing business, etc. But whatever it was, these companies know business operations. They go in, take over, and succeed where others have failed. Like good repairmen, they have those missing parts that put that defunct business back into good running condition.

DO NOT LET DETOURS THROW YOU

Keep your ultimate goal in mind. There is a great difference between a road that goes "Nowhere" and a detour that leads back to the main highway.

There is also a difference between detouring and starting over again; in starting over again, you generally have to go back to the starting point, whereas a detour is merely a little longer way around. But whether you are starting over again or taking a detour, there is one important thing to keep in mind, and that is your ultimate goal.

ALLOW YOUR INDIVIDUALITY TO HELP YOU

Many times when we enter a business venture, we have worked out a complete program. We have "checked out" all the parts that go into making a successful enterprise, but we have overlooked our own individuality, our own personality. These most valuable assets are overlooked because they are such an intimate part of each of us that we do not realize that we are an individual unlike any other person in the world.

So when you are setting up your program for a business venture, a speech at a political meeting, a talk before a ladies club at your church, or your final argument to the jury, do not forget the important part your individuality can play. It could possibly make the difference, and it probably will.

POINTS TO REMEMBER ABOUT IT IS EASIER TO SUCCEED THAN TO FAIL

- No one wants to fail. It is obviously harder to do something that is distasteful than something pleasant, and most people consider success pleasant. Take advantage of this built-in motivation to succeed.
- Failure often leads to a superior form of success. A person who has failed and finally succeeds is more likely to be aware of all of the pitfalls and dangers in his field of endeavor. Historically, many of our most creative and successful people were originally failures.
- Don't you be guilty of any of the 11 most common mistakes that lead to business failures. Be especially aware of the problems that accompany the management of a family business.

- Formulas for failure are almost non-existent; but formulas for success abound in every bookstore. Take advantage of the successes of others and find out how they did it.

- Don't be "detoured" from achieving your goals. If you take the longer way around, you may never make it.

11

Be An Individual Even When You Sleep

I can hear a slight "rumble" when the above title is read. "What do you mean, be an individual even when you sleep?" Yes, that's what the title says, and that is what the title means.

Sleeping is becoming one of America's greatest problems. Without proper rest, the next day can become a monstrosity. Pills today are big business. There are pills that are not habit-forming; there are yellow pills, red pills, and two-toned capsules. Some are under a doctor's prescription, some are not. We have pills to go to sleep, pills to get going, pills to slow you down, pills to relax you.

I cannot remember my parents or my grandparents having any sleeping problems. They were physically worn out when the day ended. Today, most of us, if we are tired, are mentally tired. Sleep is necessary to a normal life and a good day's work. Again, we must determine our sleeping habits, as individuals. We should have a program for going to sleep and getting the required number of hours' sleep. This program should be geared to us as an individual.

I know an individual who is slightly on the unusual side. I have never decided whether his unusual method of getting the required number of hours' sleep is real or purely a figment of his peculiar imagination. He always seems to be fresh, pent up with energy, and has an appearance that reflects ten hours' sleep. But he has told me confidentially on numerous occasions that he never gets over six hours' sleep, and most of the time it is closer to four. I do not believe or buy his theory, but here it is:

"I studied hypnotism for a long time," he confided in me. "Then one week when I was getting very little sleep, I said to myself, "Why couldn't I hypnotize myself at night to get eight hours sleep in four hours? So I tried it," he said. "I sat before a large mirror in my pajamas. The time was 3 A.M., and I knew I had to get up at seven. I also knew I should have eight hours' sleep to be myself and do a good day's work. So I simply hypnotized myself into getting eight hours' sleep in the next four. That was over a year ago, and it has been working beautifully for me ever since."

Whether his theory works, or he merely thinks it

works, I do not know; but we must admit, "He is an individual even when he sleeps."

The old story about the businessman who could not sleep is still a good example of how the inability to sleep is more an emotional or mental condition than a real physical problem.

Jim Brown would lie in bed at night for hours before dozing off to sleep. He didn't think that he should take a sleeping pill; and when he did, he worried so much about taking the pill that it did him very little good.

Jim lay there night after night, looking more like an owl than a businessman getting a well-deserved night of rest. Finally his doctor told him, "Jim, tonight if you do not go to sleep in the first hour after you retire, I want you to get up, put on your clothes, and take a walk. Start with a two-block walk. I want you to walk leisurely. Try not to think of anything except that you are tired, and you should be at home, in bed, sleeping. If that does not work, try four blocks tomorrow night—then six blocks, eight blocks, and so on."

Jim was up to ten blocks the night he went to bed during a driving rainstorm. He could hear the loud roar of thunder miles away. Rain with a mixture of hail beat against the window. Through his partly closed eyes streaks of lightning danced.

Then he remembered that the last time he had sent his raincoat to the cleaners it came back minus all traces of repellancy. He had planned on buying a new one, but somehow he hadn't gotten around to it. Then he thought about his rubbers—yes, his rubbers; they were down at the office. He was trying to remember where he left his umbrella when he fell off, fast asleep.

Today, with the fast tempo and pressure of modern business, we often find that the bed is not a place of rest, but merely an object that separates night and day. It is a secluded place where some of us do our best worrying as we roll and toss until the alarm beckons us to another day's work.

Sleeping—like most of our problems—is an individual problem. I believe that it is most important to analyze our own sleeping habits. And as I have suggested before, and will suggest throughout this book, *formulate an individual program for yourself.* If you have set up a loose-leaf notebook, make some notes when you finish this chapter; see if some of the ideas, problems, and suggestions pertain to you or could help you.

Lawyers who have handled divorce cases will tell you that the sleeping habits of many husbands and wives can be a contributing factor to their marital difficulties. To me, many of the idiosyncracies of the husband and wife are quite humorous; but to a couple who are balancing on the verge of divorce, they are serious. Here are a few comments made by those who were irritated by the sleeping habits of their mate.

> He drinks at least three cups of black coffee before coming to bed, while I only have a glass of warm milk. Well, I am hardly settled in bed before he's off in dreamland. I wouldn't mind that so much, but lately I just cannot doze off. So, while I

> am lying there trying to relax and go to sleep he giggles, and I know he is dreaming about me and my ridiculous glass of warm milk, as he calls it.

Here is another bed problem.

> My husband cannot sleep unless he has both arms and shoulders out of the covers. I cannot sleep unless I have the covers pulled up right under my chin. Neither of us like twin beds, so all night long it's a "tug of war."

Another story:

> I suggested that my wife and I have separate bedrooms. She now thinks I either have another woman or I don't care for her any more. The truth is, I cannot stand her sleeping equipment, which includes eye shades, a chin strap, and a smeared-on night cream that smells like a combination of rancid bacon grease and used crankcase oil. I have tried to talk to her about it, but she always counters with "How do you think you look with a day-old beard and smelling like stale beer and cheap cigars?

PREPARE FOR BED AS YOU WOULD FOR WORK

Most of us do not prepare for bed. What works for one individual does not work for the next person. So check this list to see what pertains to you as an individual. Make notes of the things you feel might help you. Be realistic, be honest with yourself.

1. Do not indulge in either food or drink before retiring.
2. Avoid anything that might upset you emotionally—T.V. horror shows, murder mysteries, arguments.
3. Do not rehash unpleasant things that happened during the day.
4. Try listening to soft, pleasant music in a semidark room.
5. If you have a difficult day confronting you tomorrow, get out a pad and pencil and plan a program on what you will do, when you will do it, and how it will be done. Put the things down in the order of their importance. Once you have completed the program, forget it until the next morning.
6. Find out what kind of mattress suits you best.
7. Determine how to ventilate your bedroom without having a draft, particularly in the fall and winter months.
8. What do you wear to bed? Individuals who wear little, especially in the fall and winter, will find that this can be the cause of back and shoulder aches.

   (*Note:* It has been recommended by certain doctors that, starting in October, everyone should wear a light cotton turtleneck jersey under his pajamas or sleeping gown. I have been doing this for five years and have found that it has eliminated most of the pains and aches that heretofore I had during the fall and winter months. The theory behind this is that at night when the room is cool some of us will perspire some on the side we are lying on. Then when one rolls over and the cool or cold air reaches the warm and sometimes "clammy" pajamas, this causes the muscles to tighten. A spastic muscle can affect the nerves, cause aches and bothersome pain. When the spring comes around, a "T" shirt is substituted for the turtleneck jersey, and with summer it's back to just P.J.'s until October. The part that the turtleneck jersey plays in this program is that it absorbs any perspiration while the cool or cold air only reaches the outside of the pajamas; the back, shoulders, and neck being kept warm by the inner garment.)

9. Try to feel that you have done a good day's work and deserve a good night's sleep, and that you are even going to do better tomorrow.
10. Your night garments should reflect your individualism. Do not wear something or some color merely because someone else thinks you should.
11. Sometimes a little lotion will give you a feeling of well-being.
12. It is said that the best sleeping position is on your right side with your right leg straight and your left knee brought up to a half bend, but I say sleep in any position that suits you.
13. Give a little thought to your sleeping habits, and above all—*Be an individual even when you sleep.*

A WARM BATH AND A LIGHT SNACK SOMETIMES MAKE THE DIFFERENCE

A warm bath can relax you. A light snack will divert some of the blood from your brain to your stomach. The combination of these two can induce sleepiness.

What do I consider a light snack? That is a very good question. It is another one of those questions that you will have to ask yourself and formulate your own answer.

I believe that we can agree that what might be a light snack for one person could be a meal for another. Let's take a 120-pound office worker and compare him to a 235-pound truck driver or a football player. I am sure that what would be considered a light snack for the football player wouldn't be exactly a light snack for the office worker.

There are some things you should know about when you peek in that refrigerator around midnight and you are getting ready to "whip up" that "light snack."

First, you should know something about calories and what foods are high in calories.

Second, to maintain a certain weight, use the "theory of fifteen."

EXAMPLE: If you want to maintain a weight of 150 pounds, and you do an ordinary day's work, it will usually take 2250 calories per day. This is arrived at by multiplying 15×150. If you would like to lose about four pounds a month, subtract 500 calories a day from the 2250; and if you wish to add a few pounds a month, add 500 calories per day.

Third, in trying to arrive at what constitutes a midnight snack for you, you should consider the following:

a. Have you eaten or drunk more than usual during the last six hours?

b. Have you had anything to drink or eat during the last two or three hours?

c. Are you on a diet, under a doctor's care, overweight or underweight?

If after checking all of the above, you cannot figure what a light snack should consist of for you, well, warm up half a glass of fortified skimmed milk with a thin piece of toast as a side order.

LEAVE YOUR UNFINISHED PROBLEMS FOR THE NEXT DAY

We must accept the fact that each day will have its problems. What we haven't done about the problems we failed to solve today, and the ones that will confront us tomorrow, should be put to sleep at bedtime.

Try to think of something pleasant when you lie down. If you have done a good day's work, you deserve a good night's rest. Tomorrow will probably be with you before you are ready. A good night's sleep will condition you to solve today some of those unsolved problems of yesterday.

KEEP A PAD AND PENCIL OR A TAPE RECORDER BY YOUR SIDE

One of the disturbing things that will keep you from going to sleep and keep you from going back to sleep when you wake up during the night is:

To suddenly remember something you forgot during the day.
To get an idea about something you have been trying to get an idea about for over a week.
To remember something that you are afraid you won't remember tomorrow.

A pencil and pad or a tape recorded will let you make a record of your thoughts and go right off to sleep.

DON'T WORRY IF YOU HAVE A SLEEPLESS NIGHT

All of us at some time or other have a bad night. Fretting or worrying about it only makes it worse. Bring out your humor, laugh about it. Use your positive attitude. Positive thinkers feel that if they have a sleepless night tonight, they will drop off fast the next night and sleep right through until morning.

If you have an unusually bad night, get up, make yourself a cup of tea, and listen to some soft, dreamy music. Think of something pleasant until you get drowsy.

POINTS TO REMEMBER ABOUT BEING AN INDIVIDUAL WHEN YOU SLEEP

- You need the proper amount of rest each night. The "proper amount" varies from individual to individual; hence, you should tailor a sleep program to fit your own rest needs.
- Husbands and wives are often irritated by their spouse's sleeping habits. See if you can't correct sleeping habits that might be disturbing your wife or husband.
- Going to bed requires about as much preparation as does going to work; yet, most people do very little in the way of preparing for bed. Follow the general suggestions that are found in this chapter and make them conform to your special needs.
- If you have problems, do not take them to bed with you. Instead, before you go to bed, formulate a plan of attack for solving your most pressing problems the next day. Then, forget all about your troubles and get a good night of sleep.
- Have a pad and pencil or a tape recorder near your bed. If you get a "Brainstorm" during the night, you can keep a record of it and easily fall off to sleep again, knowing that it is safely recorded for later reference.

12

Individual Confidence Destroys Fear

Without confidence, fear begins to breed. It can start with unwarranted concern; this concern can develop into worry; and worry into real FEAR.

FEAR WILL WARP YOUR JUDGMENT

You will find that you will reach a point where you are afraid to make the smallest decisions. You will imagine the most horrible things that can happen to you no matter what you decide; and if you do not make a decision, you worry about what will happen because you did not make a decision.

I once heard a sermon given by a father on confidence and fear. His explanation covered the subject so completely I have been unable to improve upon it. He said:

> To see how fear not only warps your judgment but destroys all confidence along with it, let's consider the following example: We will take a plank 14 inches wide, 2 inches thick and 15 feet long. We will place this board on two cement blocks 8 inches high. You are now asked to walk across the room on this board. If you do, you will receive $100. For $100 all you have to do is walk 15 feet on a board 14 inches wide that is only 8 inches off the floor. This you would like to do all day long. You have great confidence. There isn't the slightest trace of fear. Now we take the same board up to the 32nd story and place this 15-foot board between two buildings. We also raise the "ante" to $300 to walk across the same board—the same 15 feet. The only difference is instead of 8 inches from the floor, it is now about one block to the street. You look at the board—you stare at the street down below. All you can say is, "No thanks." Your confidence has disappeared. Fear has completely warped your judgment. You cannot put one foot in front of the other on the same 14-inch board that you glided across with ease when it was only 8 inches off the floor.

Confidence is often a very different thing to different individuals. Confidence is natural for some, and in others it must be cultivated. Each of us must build our own confidence. And once we build it, it becomes a real part of us, and it will dispel any fear. But many say,

"Those are nice words, but how do you build this confidence? What are the components that make up this vital trait? Where does one start, and where do you go from there?"

I do not believe that confidence is a single trait or a simple condition of the mind. It is made up of many factors. It includes courage, know-how, ability, spirit, self-reliance. It is built upon trial and error, effort, enthusiasm, and the feeling of wanting to accomplish something.

Let's take a simple example to start with. Bobby Jones was five years old when his father thought it was about time that he learned to swim. Bobby's experience with water was limited to the bathtub. When his dad took him over to the municipal swimming pool, he spent most of his first hour hanging on to his father's neck and yelling, "No, please Daddy, don't put me down."

It was during the second hour that Daddy persuaded Bobby to hold his breath while Daddy held his; and with Bobby's arms clinched around Daddy's neck, they both ducked their heads, but only for a second—then for two seconds, then for five.

By the time that Bobby visited the pool three times, he had enough confidence to duck his own head if, of course, Daddy had a tight hold on him and pulled him up at the count of five.

From ducking himself, Bobby learned to paddle and kick, provided of course that Daddy held on to his swimming suit and raised him out of the water every time his head went under.

Then came the day when Bobby was going to try to swim from the side of the pool to his daddy ten feet away. He made three false starts before he started for his daddy. His teeth were clinched; he held his breath; he kicked his feet; and he paddled his arms with all of his strength. Water churned in all directions. Bobby couldn't see his daddy because his head was tucked tightly against his chest, and his eyes were closed. Daddy seemed to be miles away instead of just ten feet. Then Bobby felt himself being lifted out of the water and his father excitingly saying, "You made it, Bobby, you made it all by yourself."

From that first ten-foot swim, Bobby progressed to swimming the width of the pool, then to diving. Of course, the diving was more like a log rolling off a one-foot bank. To Bobby, it was diving.

Before the summer ended, Bobby was diving (as he called it) from the low diving board and swimming the length of the pool. He never walked back, but ran, to get back on that diving board to dive again and again with all of the confidence that any five-year-old could possess.

This was the same Bobby who four short months ago hung desperately to his daddy pleading, "Please, Daddy, please don't put me down."

In this story of Bobby we have the component parts that make up *Individual Confidence That Destroys Fear.*

First, he had real fear, with no trace of confidence.

Why? Because Bobby at this point did not have

experience or know-how. The fact that he saw other boys swimming and having fun did not in the least impress him; his fear had warped any idea of fun.

Second, he did not develop confidence in a split second. His father led him very gently into accepting the initial ducking, while he held him securely.

Third, Bobby was not being led into something beyond his capacity.

Fourth, it was not until he did the same thing over and over again that his individual confidence destroyed fear.

Fifth, each time he swam a little farther, he had more confidence and less fear.

To develop confidence, you must have desire; you must be willing to expend the effort and time to gain the experience that is needed to make you feel at ease. As stated before, you should have a program to follow —a program that has been formulated for you as an individual. And, above all, you must profit by your mistakes when it becomes necessary to start over, and possibly over and over again.

One of the fears that I hear the most is, "I just cannot get up and make a talk; I go all to pieces merely thinking of it," or "For some reason when I am called on in a meeting I never seem to be able to contribute anything to the discussion. I am so scared I am going to say something wrong that I generally don't say anything at all."

I believe that we can agree that the ability to make a

short talk or a speech—to express oneself in an individual and interesting manner—is not only a great asset but a road to recognition and an avenue to success.

I also believe that examples that we can interpret in our own individual way, to fit into our own particular personality and mannerisms, are better than instruments, guides, or patterns. I always have the feeling when I read what I should or must do that I am back in school with my textbooks.

Examples that I can study, examples which afford me the opportunity to place myself, with my personality, my individualism, in a like position, give me the opportunity to develop my own style, my own program for handling such situations when and if they arise.

I was once asked, "How can a person with a squeaky voice like mine ever make an interesting talk?"

I answered this person with another question, "Did you ever hear any of the following speak: Andy Devine, "Satchmo" Armstrong, "Snozzle" Durante? If you have, I am sure you knew you were not listening to an English commentator. But these individuals took advantage of their voices and went on to great fame.

Occasionally I hear, "How does one who is not used to making a speech start developing a program for writing, editing, and delivering a short talk?" I could have told this individual some of the things I have read and heard like

> When you start to prepare a speech, be sure you know ten times more about your subject than you deem will be necessary.

> Write and rewrite your speech at least ten times before you accept the final draft.
>
> Memorize your speech from beginning to end so you will not be at a loss for words, etc.

But, to me, these well meant suggestions are of little or no help, and in some instances can be a hindrance or a drawback.

Here is a story, an example, that should answer some of the above questions.

Bob Webster lived in the suburbs west of Chicago. He was an ordinary person with no unusual traits that would make him outstanding in any group or crowd.

He worked for an insurance firm where he reviewed claims, checked investigations, and gathered statistics. The only club he belonged to was the "Couple's Club," a husband-and-wife club. Bob would have avoided this also, but his wife insisted they join. The club had over 75 members and met once a month. The purpose was to keep up on current events, discuss local problems, and exchange ideas. The program committee selected a speaker from the group along with a topic for each meeting.

At the last meeting, the topic was "What to Do About the Increase of Burglaries and Robberies in Our Village." The evening ended with a discussion of the use of police dogs. The program committee selected Bob as the speaker for the next meeting. The topic was "The Use of Police Dogs in the Field of Security."

Bob tried every maneuver he knew to avoid the assignment, and twice he thought he had it made. In the end, all he was able to accomplish was a month's continuance.

Now, let's take a second look at Bob. He had never given a talk before a group. He always felt ill at ease when called upon for his opinion. He never owned a dog, and if it was really known, he had an inward feeling that dogs did not like him. Once he had a dream about being kidnapped by a group of neighborhood dogs. They took him to their leader, a large German Shepherd. It was all so realistic. The huge police dog sat on some kind of a throne, and he wore a checked sport coat and a bright, orange pair of slacks. Bob could still remember that the big dog kept repeating,

> What right have you to be a man and eat at a nice clean table while I must eat out of a dirty bowl. I am smarter than you, and you know it; so I repeat, what right have you?

Robert Webster is now a worried, unhappy individual. He does not have a program. The little confidence he had is now gone. Fear has warped his judgment. He is beginning to despise himself, hate dogs, and as far as that Couple's Club—well, the club can just get along without the Websters.

Before Bob becomes an uninteresting, unhappy introvert, we had better start changing his thinking. First, we remind him that he has always liked the Couple's Club, and that he had met some of his best friends there. Remember last year when the Websters and the Conroys went on that fishing trip in Canada? Do you recall the talk that Jim Conroy gave on fishing for lake trout in Canada? Remember how you enjoyed hearing him tell about the big lake trout that you caught? And you couldn't help noticing how popular Jim grew after that talk.

And now, you have even a bigger opportunity than Jim had. Yes, that's right, a bigger opportunity. How come? Well, to begin with, everyone is not interested in fishing, but everyone is interested in his home, his possessions. To add to this interest is the alarm caused by the recent increase in robberies and burglaries. Besides, who can resist a friendly, panting, tail-wagging dog?

Bob is not convinced at this point that he can even get up before the Couple's Club and just say hello, but he has started to realize that he is going to have to make some kind of a talk.

He always likes to do a good job. He would like to be more personable, to make his wife proud of him. But now at least he is beginning to think in a positive way.

As yet, he has no plan, and his enthusiasm is drooping. He hasn't the slightest idea where to start. He has seven weeks to prepare a thirty-minute talk, but he wishes it were seven years.

His wife suggested he ask some of his friends where he could find something, anything, about police dogs. He finally asked a Chicago police captain, who briefed him on the Canine Division of the Chicago Police, and who suggested he write to the Canine Division of the Police Department of St. Louis.

The Metropolitan Police Department of the City of St. Louis, which had started using dogs on October 13,

1958, sent Bob an eleven-page brief on their experience with the use of dogs. This started the little flame under Bob's enthusiasm. As he read and digested the report, the flame burned brighter. He now started making notes for his speech.

When he went back to thank the police captain who had suggested he write to the Canine Division of the St. Louis Police Department, the captain made another suggestion: "Why don't you go out to the kennel on the west side where the police dogs are trained? Tell the gentleman in charge I sent you."

Reluctantly, Bob went out. The trainer had just started to train a German Shepherd named Sparky. This dog was being trained for a new type of assignment. When his training was completed, he would be assigned with a handler to a four-story warehouse. Unlike other police dogs, this dog was not being taught to attack. His duties would be to make hourly trips through the warehouse. On each floor there would be two stations. The dog would stop at each station. If the dog could not detect by smell any living object, he pushed a pedal. This would register in the guardhouse. The dog would also wear a light harness with a two-way radio connected. He would respond to orders and give certain warnings by barking. The trainer suggested Bob work with this young dog.

The flame of enthusiasm was now burning bright. Bob was fascinated by the new world he had entered. He went out to the kennel twice a week. Sparky seemed to like him. From a very simple start of merely walking Sparky, Bob progressed with the dog. Sparky would "sit" on command, and walk properly at heel with or without a leash. Also, on command, Sparky would not only sit but "down" and "stay" on command.

When Bob had gathered all of his notes, he had enough material for five speeches. He knew all about the use of dogs in England. He studied the different breeds of dogs—the Bloodhound, the Labrador, the Doberman, the Rottweiler, the German Shepherd. He noted the special qualities of each breed and why the German Shepherd was considered the best for police work.

His notes included detailed information on the training of the German Shepherd for different types of security assignments. He had pages on the sense of smell, sense of hearing, air scent, and psychological effect of dogs.

Bob had read somewhere about preparing a speech with the use of a tape recorder. He borrowed a tape recorder. He was disappointed with the way he sounded, so he rearranged his notes and tried again. He did not sound the way he felt.

He asked one of the boys down at the office, who was noted for after-dinner talks, to help him. He helped him by putting Bob's words on his tape recorder. Bob tried again. He listened to his friend's recording, noting the timing, pausing, and emphasis put on certain words and phrases.

By the time Bob had recorded and re-recorded his talk eight times, all fear had disappeared. Individual confidence had taken over.

Before the eventful night for Bob's talk came around, he remembered reading somewhere, "Don't be afraid to be different." So when the evening came around and the clock showed 8:30, the time for his talk, he was nowhere around. It was 8:35 when Bob made his entrance with Sparky, a well trained and behaved dog. Sparky stood by as Bob began to talk:

> Sorry that my friend here and I are late, but we thought it advisable to circle the block to be sure that there were no loiterers sneaking around who were not members of our Couple's Club. I would like to introduce my friend, a purebred German Shepherd whose name is Sparky. Would you say hello to the folks here by barking twice?

Sparky barked deep and loud.

> And now Sparky, will you back up about three steps, sit, and stay sit while I tell the members of the Couple Club what you and your relatives are doing to protect property, people, and personal belongings in the Chicago area.

Sparky never moved during Bob's thirty-minute talk. On command, he barked three times to say good-bye, and then, walking proudly at heel, followed Bob down the center aisle. The applause they received still rang in Bob's ears hours later.

Now, let's analyze what happened here. Bob started out with two fears: his dread of facing his friends and giving a talk and his fear of dogs. He was forced into doing something after all efforts to avoid making a speech had failed. Once he was convinced there was no way out, he proceeded to work out a program. Step by step, his confidence grew until when the night he feared arrived, the confidence he had developed destroyed all fear.

When we stop and analyze fear and take a good look at confidence, we should do it as an individual. The fears of one person are not necessarily the fears of another. The confidence needed by one individual to destroy fear will not be the same as needed by another.

"So what," you will say, "each of us needs a different kind of confidence. But how do we get that kind of confidence, and where do we start?"

I would say that our very first step is to determine whether or not the fear is real. If you are afraid the world is going to end or that it will rain during your vacation, you are concerning yourself with things you cannot do anything about. So, just forget about them. There are enough things you *can* do something about, and confidence will be needed there.

The next step is to find out why we are afraid—what do we fear? Here are a few negative things to check:

1. No experience.
2. Looking for the worst to happen.
3. Not realizing your own capabilities.
4. No desire to achieve.
5. No enthusiasm.
6. Unwarranted concern.
7. Unwilling to expend the effort.
8. Not feeling important.
9. A defeatist attitude before you start.
10. Wanting to quit at the first detour.

Now let's check a few positive things:

1. Willing to spend the time and effort to gain the experience and know-how that will give you the courage to proceed to point of confidence.
2. Realizing the satisfaction of achieving your ultimate goal.
3. Seeking advice and help from others when needed.
4. Working out a step-by-step program.
5. Releasing the things within yourself that are held back by fear.
6. Bring out your own individual humor.
7. Keep a written record of your progress and your problem.
8. Develop proper mental attitude.
9. Be inspired. See what others have done, you can do the same.

CONTROL YOUR EMOTIONS—DON'T LET THEM CONTROL YOU

Without emotions, life would not be worthwhile. But, like every other thing, there is a time and place for them. Emotions can be "all-inspiring" or completely frustrating. However, they know very little about control. Like individuals, emotions are different in character and in depth.

Before you can control your emotions, you should know something about them. Otherwise, it will be like trying to fly an airplane without any instructions.

First, make an honest and complete examination of yourself.
Second, make a list of those emotions you feel you enjoy and that you can control.
Third, list those that seem to have a tendency to control you.
Fourth, see what you can do to transfer those emotions on the second list to the first list.

Once you have your emotions under control, it will help increase your confidence.

THE MORE YOU KNOW ABOUT YOURSELF, THE GREATER YOUR CONFIDENCE

Confidence is the result of many things. One of the most important is knowing all about yourself.

Know your capacity.
Know your limitations.
Know when you should "stand pat."
Know when you should compromise.
Know all about every venture before you start.
Know what to expect and what it might demand of you.
Know when to ask for help and how to get it.

HAVE FAITH IN YOURSELF

Faith in yourself is very close to confidence in yourself. I explain the difference this way: Faith is the same as confidence, except when you have faith in yourself, you have that additional feeling that God is on your side.

IT IS BETTER TO HAVE PEOPLE ENJOY YOU THAN FEEL SORRY FOR YOU

Confidence is one of the traits that attracts people. If you are a fisherman, it is the guide with that certain gleam of confidence that you want for that fishing trip. It is the doctor with that reassuring smile. It is the butcher that holds up that rib roast as though he has been saving it just for you. It is the lawyer who looks straight at you, and in a firm unmistakable voice, says "You have nothing to worry about." It is these individuals who draw you to them.

When you have confidence, and it shows, people will want to be associated with you. They will enjoy your company, and you cannot help having a certain feeling of satisfaction. But, if you lack confidence, if you do very little but complain, if you keep changing your mind without reason, people might feel sorry for you, but they will not seek your company.

POINTS TO REMEMBER ABOUT GAINING INDIVIDUAL CONFIDENCE TO DESTROY FEAR

- Fear can destroy a person's sense of judgment; it can paralyze effective action. The best way to erase fear from your life is to build up confidence to a point where it drives fear out.

- To develop confidence, you should have a program that is backed up by real desire to rid your life of unfounded fears. This program must incorporate measures that will give you experience in the areas of your fears—we fear less those things which are known.

- Here again, use the example method to overcome your fears—gain confidence from the example of others who have conquered their fears.

- You should control your emotions—not be controlled by them. This self-mastery will help in building your confidence.

- In the same way, the more you know about yourself, the more confidence you will have, the more faith you will have in yourself. Don't be the kind of person that people pity.

13

You Can Learn Something From Everyone

Once, after making the statement, "You can learn something from everyone," I was challenged by a young man who said:

"I work for the most miserable boss who ever lived. He's tactless; he hasn't the slightest interest in anyone in the office. He gloats when he catches you making a mistake, and only mumbles when you come up with a good idea. If his uncle wasn't the majority stockholder, he couldn't hold a job in the stockroom. Now, just what am I supposed to learn from this character?"

I merely looked at him for a second. "Don't you really know?" I asked.

"You mean I should learn how not to be like that?"

He had answered his own question. In the conversation that followed he told me more details about his boss. Near the end of our talk, I suggested that he make notes of all the wrong and tactless things his boss did during the month and then write down suggestions on how he would have handled the situations or what he would have said and how he would have said it. When I met him later, he told me that he had developed my suggestion into a game. I didn't ask him about the details of the game, but it was easy to see he was learning something and enjoying every minute of it.

Of all that can be written about learning something from everyone, there is one rule that is a must—BE OBSERVANT. Develop curiosity, because curiosity leads to observing. And, if you add a little of your own personality to what you see, hear, and learn, it will go a long way in helping you to be an individual 24 hours a day.

I think one of the best examples of "you can learn something from everyone" is the story that has been told many times about the large trailer truck that got wedged under a viaduct. While the mechanics and experts were trying to figure out how to get the huge trailer out without damaging the truck or the viaduct, a small 7-year-old boy, licking an all-day sucker said, "Mister, why don't you let some of the air out of the tires so you can back it out?"

So, from children, from animals, even from people you do not particularly agree with, you can learn something.

DON'T COPY, BUT LEARN TO ADOPT THE THINGS THAT FIT IN WITH YOUR PERSONALITY

As you observe personality traits in other people, analyze your own individuality and determine whether or not you can adopt some of the things you observe. So many of us see, but we do not *observe.*

For those of you who have set up a loose-leaf notebook, let us study attitudes for the next month; not our own, but attitudes of others, both good and bad.

Observe the following and make notes:

Tact
Appreciation
Sincerity
Humor
Understanding
Sportsmanship
Friendliness
Honesty
Likes and dislikes
Adaptability
Flexibility

The main purpose of doing this is to get you to observe. We cannot learn if we do not develop the ability to observe.

If you will observe the attitudes of your family, your friends, and your business associates for a one-month period, you will find you will be surprised how many of their traits you were not consciously aware of and how many you did not recognize as traits either good or bad, but merely as an intricate part of the individual.

I was born with a natural curiosity which led to the ability to observe things that other people did not seem to see. As an example of observing, coupled with "you can learn something from everyone," I had an unusual experience many years ago while on a fishing trip near Ludington, Michigan.

The camp was loaded with fly fishermen. They had the latest in everything—wet flies, dry flies, big flies, little flies, and some homemade flies. Most of them could handle their fly rods with the precision of a sculptor. Many of them could whip a fly into a hat 60 feet away.

Every day, these "well-equipped" and experienced fishermen started out for their favorite trout stream. But somehow the trout were not impressed. The catches were small and limited.

No one seemed to pay much attention to an old Indian who usually sat around doing nothing. I missed him one day, and then I noticed him coming through the woods with a string of the nicest trout I had seen. It wasn't difficult to notice he was sneaking back to camp and had no idea of showing off or displaying his catch.

Three days later when the sun was high and the camp was deserted, I saw the old Indian slip out of camp. I got my binoculars and followed him. I knew at his age he did not see too well, so it was easy to keep out of sight.

About a half-mile from camp, he stopped. After making sure no one was watching him, he became a very busy Indian with a long knife he had tucked in his belt. He began to cut sections of bark about 5 inches square from several trees. Then he started digging around the base of these trees. He took a red bandana handkerchief from his pocket and put the grub worms that he dug into the handkerchief. He stood up to be sure he was not being watched and took one last look around. Then he set out for a stream a half a block away.

The stream at this point had made several short bends which slowed it down as it ducked under a 100-foot overhanging underbrush.

Through the binoculars, I could see very plainly what he was doing at the edge of the bank at the point where the stream ducked under the overhanging brush. He was putting a grub worm on the hook attached to a roll of line he had retrieved from his back pocket. On one of the pieces of bark he placed the squirming grub. He gently placed the small piece of bark in the water, allowing it to float slowly under the overhanging brush. I could see him feeding out the line. Then a quick tug of the line, and the grub left its floating raft. A trout, which had been hiding from the high noon sun, soon hit it. Five times the old Indian prepared his floating raft. Five times he pulled out a beautiful trout. Then he rolled up his line, tucked his knife away, put his lovely trout on a stringer, and sneaked back to camp.

I never mentioned the old Indian's private fishing hole to anyone. But I learned something about catching trout that day without the benefit of the latest equipment and the ability to whip a fly 60 feet into a hat.

ALWAYS TAKE A SECOND LOOK

It is difficult to learn something with just one quick glance.

I never paid much attention to ants until one night while on my way to Florida I stopped at a new motel in Opelika, Alabama. I had planned to stop in Columbus, but a driving rain changed my plans.

I wanted to leave early the next morning, and knowing that there would be little chance of getting any breakfast at that early hour, I had bought some sweet rolls and had gotten a thermos full of hot coffee. I was most surprised at five o'clock the next morning when I went over to the small table where I had placed my box of sweet rolls. There were hundreds of ants coming across the table two abreast, crawling up the side of my sweet roll box, ducking inside, and coming out again.

As I drank my hot coffee without the benefit of a sweet roll, I took a second look. I traced the marching line up and down the leg of the table, then across the floor to the bathroom. Here these little creatures circled the bathroom, marching close to the wall to a small hole on the opposite side.

My first thought was, if they were smart enough to find those sweet rolls in the blackness of the night, wake up all of their sisters and brothers, and set up a well organized production line, then why did they want to lug that tiny piece of sugar all the way around the room when they could cut directly across? And then it came.

From past experience, they must have found out that at various times of the night people, some with big feet, run in and out of that bathroom; and probably one night a couple who had been drinking gave that bathroom a real workout, stamping out 500 of their marching workers.

Before I left the motel, I tossed the box in the waste basket. Before I checked out, I went back and took a third look. They were still marching up the leg to the table top where there was great confusion. I could almost hear them say, "What happened? Where did it go? Someone has to go back to headquarters and tell Big Joe to stop the marchers. Somebody has fouled us up."

As I drove away I couldn't help but think what a great job of organization and perfect discipline, with everybody working. But when the objective was moved, and their ultimate goal disappeared, they were much like us humans—a confused lot.

YOU CAN EVEN LEARN FROM ANIMALS AND INSECTS

We are now beginning to study animals, birds, insects—and we are learning, but not always understanding.

Turtles, snakes, and the like, hibernate. We do not know exactly how this is accomplished. If we did, many of us would sleep through the winter.

Studying the lightning bug, whose rear light glows bright without heat, has been a help in developing our lights.

So when you see a bird watcher, don't think he is a bit odd. Remember, he is not only enjoying himself; he could be learning something.

RECOGNIZE THE MISTAKES OF OTHERS AS WELL AS THEIR SUCCESS

Too often, we merely want to look at the good things. But unless we look at the bad, we do not have anything to use as a measure for comparison.

It is not only wise to observe the mistakes, but to look at the results of these mistakes. Far too often, we dismiss the failures and mistakes of others without giving much thought to why they failed or why the mistakes were made. By analyzing the mistakes of others, you can learn many things you cannot learn reviewing their successes.

TAKE A LOOK AT YOUR LEARNING POWER

Some of us look but never see. Others see but do not observe. Others observe but never learn, and some even learn and never use their learnings.

Suggestions: Try observing something different, something unusual, and see if you can possibly learn anything from it. If you have a group of close friends, have each one look up something that none of you know very much about and have open discussion on the matter. It can be interesting, fun, and many times, beneficial.

POINTS TO REMEMBER ABOUT LEARNING SOMETHING FROM EVERYONE

- You must be OBSERVANT to learn something from everyone. To become observant, you must develop curiosity.
- You can learn these traits by observing others. This does not mean that you should copy others blindly; rather, you should adapt methods used by others to fit in with your individual personality traits.
- It is a good policy to look twice at things. With the rapid pace of modern life, we tend to miss much that would prove valuable. Be different and observe things that other people miss in the rush.
- Stretch your learning power. Consciously try to extend your capacity to learn from events and things around you. Remember my experience with the ants—nothing, really, is too small or too insignificant to provide a lesson for living.

14

How to Make Individual Decisions

The ability to observe and learn, coupled with the ability to make individual decisions, is very simple—but one of the most powerful formulas I know of. As our world becomes more complicated, as decisions become more numerous and far-reaching, they become more important.

The tools that each person uses to help himself or herself make decisions may vary. But there are a few basic rules that good, individual "Decision Makers" employ. Here they are:

1. Never make a decision that should be made by someone else.

2. Do not make a decision unless you have all of the facts.
3. If you have all of the facts and the decision is yours to make, make it. Do not put it off.
4. Do not make excuses if your decision happens to be wrong. Use the experience for the next time.
5. Above all, have confidence in your own ability to make decisions.

If you have a decision to make but it does not have to be made for a week, check it out with others. Put their suggestions down on paper and compare them with yours. Have the courage to alter or change your decision if you deem it advisable. But make the decision when the time comes.

The students at most law schools study what is known as "Case Law." They study actual cases in Law and Equity. This helps them to think individually when a legal problem arises in actual practice in later years. Stories and examples serve in the same manner in developing the ability to make Individual Decisions.

LITTLE DECISIONS CAN TURN OUT TO BE BIG DECISIONS

Frank Gross didn't sleep well one night. He had a 10 o'clock meeting with his boss the next morning. He had gone over and over his ideas and suggestions. A promotion would mean moving up to another level, more money, and a chance to join a country club—an opportunity to meet and entertain customers. He was a good storyteller, a good listener, and a company man. Frank knew he couldn't miss.

He dressed hurriedly the next morning and left early for the office. He thought the meeting had gone well, although the boss did not seem as friendly as he had expected. But at 10 o'clock in the morning many people do not feel friendly. Maybe he imagined things—maybe he didn't. But the promotion didn't come through. Frank never found out why he hadn't moved up, why the promotion did not materialize. Had he known, he would have been greatly embarrassed.

Two small decisions lost him the promotion—the first, to wear the suit he had worn the day before; and the second, just grabbing any tie off the tie rack without deciding what tie blended with his suit.

During the meeting, the boss heard only half of Frank's ideas. Being a meticulous dresser, he couldn't take his eyes off the grease spot on Frank's lapel and the tie that clashed with Frank's suit.

Remember the story about the good worker in the produce warehouse. He was always there first in the morning and last to leave at night. When one of the supervisors became sick, the foreman transferred Sam to supervise the unloading of two carloads of potatoes.

Sam knew that the potatoes had to be sorted in three bins. The big ones went in bin one, the small ones in bin two, and the bad or partly bad into bin three.

An hour after Sam became a temporary supervisor he was back in the boss's office. Mopping his brow and tugging at his cap, he blurted out "Please sir, I do not wanna be a supervisor."

"What is the matter, Sam?"

"Decisions, boss, decisions. Every potato needs a decision. It is a big one and goes in bin one? Is it a little one for bin two? Then after you decide that, you gotta decide if it is good enough to stay out of bin three. Please boss, put me back on my old job."

Although this is only a story, Sam made one individual decision. He had all of the facts, and it was his responsibility. That decision was that he did not want a job made up of so many decisions.

Experience, confidence, and the courage of one's convictions go a long way in helping all of us make good individual decisions.

If you will turn to the Yellow Pages in the Chicago phone book, you will find a growing list of business counselors, management consultants and business engineers. Then there are others like personnel evaluation, conduct surveys, aptitude tests, pre-employment screening, etc. Most of these services render opinions based upon decisions made by their specialists. These opinions are based upon facts uncovered in their surveys. A field representative of a large management consultant firm told me this story.

A medium sized firm located in Nashville, Tennessee, had been losing money during the past three years. It manufactured a competitive product. Its location was near its market, and transportation was excellent. It enjoyed a good labor supply and good labor relations. The general manager was an unusually young man, a football star at college, a hard worker, and a devoted company man. But when it was all added up, the net result was "Net Profits" in the red column. In an attempt to change this trend, the company decided to hire a nationally known business engineering firm to check all operations.

Two field men of the business engineering company spent two weeks checking out every operation. It was during the second week that the first inkling of what was wrong showed its head—*poor timing.* Checking out poor timing led to the office of the General Manager, the unusual young man.

He was unusual in that he did not drink. He worked six days a week instead of five, and sometimes seven. Everyone else in the office and plant worked eight hours a day, but this unusual young man worked ten, sometimes twelve, and on occasion, fourteen.

He knew the business; he knew the market; he knew everything except how to make an individual decision. His desk was piled high with papers. He worked longer each day, going over these papers, sorting them, putting them in different piles. The piles grew higher, the decisions fewer.

A very simple program was worked out for the unusual, young general manager.

1. When a decision has to be made, be sure you are the one to make it.

   Note: In sorting through the piles of papers the field men found that 20 per cent of the decisions should have been made by other executives. Another 20 per cent, the General Manager should have asked for the opinion or recommendation

of others. Decisions on some matters should have been made weeks before.
2. Facts must be secured before any decision is made.
3. Most important—Once a paper is picked up, and all the facts are known, it cannot be laid down until a decision is made.
4. If a paper is picked up where all the facts are now known, immediate steps must be taken to secure the additional information.
5. All problems and other matters must be reduced to a written outline.

If you will remember, we started this chapter with some of the above suggestions. The above story shows how some of these suggestions actually work in the operation of a business. How did the unusual young manager work out? Did the company get back in the black? Is the young man working longer hours?

The company is in the black. The General Manager is working five days a week, eight hours a day. He had learned how and when to make individual decisions.

DECISIONS IN THE MAKING

Since we are all geared differently, since we are unlike any other individual, we cannot arrive at the same decision in the same allotted time. The important thing is that we come up with a good decision when we make it.

Do not spend valuable time making a decision on small or unimportant things. Let's take an example of an individual decision that has to be made on a rather unimportant matter, and an example of a decision on an important matter.

First, suppose you want to buy a fly swatter. If you visit four hardware stores, try out four or five different kinds of handles, and then spend another half hour before you decide on the one with the red handle over the blue and the yellow, then you have spent entirely too much time making the decision. But, suppose you are going to buy a home in the suburbs. You have a family of five, and you do the following:

1. You have a friend who is a contractor. You ask him to check the house from the basement to the roof. He gives you a good report on all phases of construction, wiring, plumbing, etc.
2. You check the neighborhood in all four directions to see types of homes, school accommodations, shopping area, churches, etc.
3. You visit the home first with your wife, then with your wife and children.
4. You stop in and introduce yourself to your neighbors on both sides. You find out how long they have lived there, do they plan on staying, what do they like and dislike about the community.
5. You check the price with other homes in the vicinity.
6. You hire an attorney to check the sales contract, the title, and to arrange for the financing. You have had your banker advise you about the mortgage and the down payment most suitable to you.

Oh, yes, I forgot to mention, you made your own decision after two weeks of checking out the matter. You decided to buy, and you did not spend too much time before you made this important decision.

HOW TO AVOID MAKING BAD DECISIONS

I am going to allow you to figure out this one for yourself. Get out your pencil and paper and see what you can come up with. I'll give you two suggestions. Use your past experience. Remember some of the things you read on how to make good decisions and throw them into reverse.

LOOK AT THE ULTIMATE RESULT

Before making a decision, visualize the result you are expecting. In the operations of any type of business you must have good communications. If you put a note on the bulletin board that should have been put in each pay envelope, your message might not receive the attention and understanding you expected.

When writing a letter that could cause trouble if it should be misunderstood, I always give this advice. Before you seal it and send it on its way, read it once more. Then consider the worst place this letter could end up, or the person you would least want to read it. Consider the ultimate result. Then make your decision whether to mail it. Rewrite it or file it in the waste basket.

REVIEW YOUR PAST RECORD

We learn by experience. This applies to making decisions as well as other things. Take a good look at the decisions you have made in the past, both good and bad.

See if you can detect any one thing that might have contributed to either a good or a bad decision. Here are some of the little or odd things we are unaware of that sometimes affect our decisions.

a. Making a decision about one thing when you are more concerned and half thinking about something else.
b. Making a decision when you are not feeling well.
c. Making a decision when you have had a little too much to drink.
d. Making a decision merely to impress someone or show authority.

Just one last suggestion. Keep a record of your good and bad decisions and use them to develop your ability in making good decisions in the future.

POINTS TO REMEMBER ABOUT MAKING INDIVIDUAL DECISIONS

- The ability to learn and the ability to make individual decisions make an extremely powerful formula for success.

- Follow the general rules for "Decision Makers" outlined in this chapter.

- Don't put unnecessary emphasis on small decisions; that is a waste of time. But be very sure that what you put aside as a small decision is a *small* decision. "Small" decisions have changed the course of many a life.

- Once again, in making decisions, learn the experiences of others as well as your own past experiences. Your individuality comes into play here, as everyone has a different way of making decisions; but look to the end result. Make sure you make the best decision—get the best results.

15

New Ideas Can Be as Explosive As the A-Bomb

The A-bomb, which was one of the greatest discoveries of all times, started with an idea. However, it took years of research and the tireless efforts of many individuals before it became a reality. Converting atomic energy into peaceful uses will be as exciting and explosive as its original discovery.

Ideas do not have to be as involved or as far-reaching as the A-bomb to be useful and beneficial. A simple idea developed to its fullest extent can have unlimited possibilities. For example, take the bobby-pin; it is simple in structure and found in almost every American home where there are *any* females.

And the gentlemen who thought up the simple idea of the bobby-pin made a fortune.

There are times when all of us feel that there is nothing new, that every new idea has been thought of, worked over and wrung dry. Then while we are convincing ourselves that this is true, someone comes along with the idea of the year.

Scientists now tell us if we ever learn to harness the energy contained in the oceans on our planet we could possibly supply the earth with fuel for billions of years. Not being a scientist, this seemed very unreal to me; so I asked a few simple questions. Is there any danger in accomplishing this, and how can this unleashing the sea's energy be accomplished?

Although I did not completely understand the answer to my first question, I did understand enough to realize one of the probems was how to create the required reaction without actually creating an atomic bomb.

To my second question, I got off to a good start when I understood that our oceans contain some particles which can be described as heavy hydrogen, and that under certain conditions these particles can be made to react with each other, and in doing so yield great amounts of energy.

But when I got to where the best supply of energy comes from, I started getting lost. It seems that, like a deuteron bombarding a very heavy hydrogen nucleus, the problem is one of getting heavy hydrogen particles to move at almost the speed of light, and that we have a problem of getting tritons to collide with the deuterons at tremendous speed, and that we get tritons by bombarding lithium. But then our problem is trying to get this unusual energy without creating an atomic bomb. Well, when we reached this point, I knew I would be no help whatsoever with suggestions or ideas on how to get those little particles to collide with those other particles at just the right speed to light up our homes instead of blowing them up.

In each of our lives ideas can be not only stimulating and valuable, but the difference between being just another person or an interesting, successful individual.

MAKE A WRITTEN NOTE OF EVERY WORTHWHILE IDEA THAT COMES TO YOUR MIND

Many young executives who have good ideas have the tendency to discuss their ideas before they reduce their idea to writing. Throughout this book I will remind you to work from a program—that ideas that just rest in your head might as well be dead—that problems as well as ideas should be reduced to writing. As a business consultant said, "Don't start running before you have the ball."

When we consider the power of an idea developed to its fullest potentialities, it is comparable to the embryo that develops into the egg, then into a full grown chicken. The minute beginning is far removed from the ultimate end, but it had to start somewhere. And here is where the big questions always come up, "How do you think up an idea? Where do you start? Suppose you are not an idea person—then what?"

Then, as one young man asked, "How do I get an idea? Give me something that has some substance to it —something that I can hang my hat on instead of just words. Tell me something as an individual that I can use to start an idea."

There is always the number-one requirement that you have sufficient interest and desire to want to think up and develop ideas. If you have this, then let us look at some of the things, some of the guides, some of the realms that will start you on your way.

1. Be inquisitive.
2. Be observing.
3. Recognize problems. Think about solving them. When you do, usually an idea will be born.
4. Realize the satisfaction to be gained in creating and developing ideas.
5. Work out an idea with others.
6. Study others who seem to always come up with ideas. See if you can adopt some of their techniques.
7. As we have stated before and will state again, get the idea, no matter how small, out of your head and down on paper.
8. Remember, a simple idea can develop into being as explosive as the A-bomb as far as you as an individual are concerned.

How many times have we heard, "I had a good idea, but when I got up to speak, somehow it didn't come out the way I wanted it to.'' Maybe it was only a small gathering of parents at a P.T.A. meeting or possibly an important sales meeting, or a union meeting where you wanted to express the feelings of a minority group; but somehow everything you planned to say seemed to stick in the back of your throat.

To begin with, if your ideas get stuck in your throat, you have routed them in the wrong direction. You have taken an unnecessary detour instead of the main road.

First, you should have thought out your idea, what you wanted to say and how you wanted to say it. Then you should have bypassed your throat and run your idea down your arm through your fingers on to paper. This is where you check and recheck what you want to say. Using the checked-over idea, you get out the tape recorder. You work toward sounding the way you thought you would sound when it was only an idea in your head. Now you feed the idea back to where it belongs, your tongue. Your timing is good, you have confidence. The members are listening. You can hear yourself as you heard yourself time and time again on the tape recorder.

The words are not getting stuck in your throat—you have bypassed it. When you finish, you know for the first time that idea that had been bouncing around within you for some time has gotten out and exploded like an A-bomb.

If we tried to break down the beginning of an idea, we would probably find that it started with one of the following:

A mental impression.
A notion.
A thought.
A conception.
An apprehension.
A perception.
A reflection.
An observation.
A consideration.

It could even start with a catastrophe, an emergency, or a distasteful task—or many other things.

I have often wondered if man's attempt to fly would have been so intense if there were no birds, no insects, nothing to observe with wings.

Today we have schools and courses covering almost every subject. There is hardly anything that you would like to study that someone, somewhere, isn't teaching.

However, I am not sure there is a course entitled "Ideas for executives, housewives, students, etc., a course that is directed to each person as an individual."

The course would cover everything associated with ideas from the embryo stage to a fully completed and workable project.

MAKE WRITTEN NOTES OF ALL OF YOUR IDEAS THAT ARE WORTHWHILE

An idea that rests in your head might as well be dead. When you think, get out the paper and pencil. At times, we all feel that we will remember the idea, or we will make a note of it when we have had a little more time to think it out. Then the idea that might have developed into something big finds itself pushed aside by other ideas. These other ideas need a thought or two, and just as soon as we have time to think them out, we will reduce these ideas to writing.

MOST JOBS CAN BE DONE EASIER, FASTER, AND AT LESS COST

One of the "cry words" in business today is "Reduce Overhead," "Cut Costs," "Automation will do it faster and cheaper." Here is where the idea man or woman moves ahead.

One of the problems most of us have is that we are so busy doing the job that has to be done that we do not have the time, or want to take the time, to see how the job can be done easier, faster, or cheaper.

It is not unusual for a person from a department to come up with an idea, a good, workable idea, that pertains to another department. He has noticed the confusion in the other department. He has watched the turmoil, the frustration during certain peak periods. He asked a few questions, and then wondered why someone did not think of changing the operation. This was the beginning of the birth of an idea.

If you are an executive, a foreman, or a worker, spend some time in studying all the components of the operation of your department. See if the proper personnel are assigned to the job they are suited for. See if there are any bugs in the operations. Are there side roads used instead of the main highway? See what other firms are doing. Study all available information on the subject. Get out your pencil and paper and see what new idea you can develop.

BIG CORPORATIONS ARE LOOKING FOR IDEA MEN AND WOMEN

This topic should carry its own message. Today, competition is so great. The margin of profit between competitors is so close that an idea on packaging, on advertising, or a unique T.V. commercial can make the difference. All of these are the results of ideas. You will never know how good your ideas are until you get them down on paper, look at them from all angles, set them up in a different and attractive manner, and then select the right time to make your presentation.

CASH REWARDS FOR IDEAS BY LARGE CORPORATIONS

Many national corporations, realizing the importance of ideas, have set up suggestion boxes and idea contests. It is well proven that an idea can come from any person, regardless of his position.

The cash reward that the individual receives depends upon the value of the idea. Some of the ideas submitted are of such value that the reward runs into the thousands. This will give you an idea of how important it is to get your ideas out of your head and down on paper.

DEVELOP YOUR OWN IDEA PROGRAM

At the beginning of this book it was stated that the minute you were born you became an individual unlike any other person. You therefore think a little differently from any other person. That is why you should develop your own idea program.

Review all of the things you do, whether you be a housewife, an executive, a worker, a student, or whatever you might be. See if you cannot think of at least one idea about some of the work you are doing that might be done a little differently, a little more easily.

I have a rule that helped me. Any time I find something that I dislike doing, I try to figure out how I might do it to make it likeable or easier; and if I don't, I look for someone who likes that particular type of work or challenge and get it detailed to him.

POINTS TO REMEMBER ABOUT DEVELOPING NEW IDEAS

- Pay attention to *any* new ideas that you may have. Ideas do not have to be elaborate and complex to be valuable. In fact, the best ideas are often surprisingly simple.

- Make a policy of writing down every worthwhile idea you may have. It is a mistake to discuss your potentially important ideas before you have written them down and thought them out.

- Follow the general suggestions in this chapter for developing your ideas. Realize the great power of new ideas and the rewards that are available to those who can produce them.
- Develop your own idea program. Do this in relation to the proposition that there is an easier way to do almost every job.

16

If Your Brain Could Only Talk

What an individual—what a success we could all be—if that brain of ours could only talk! If it could only store up all of the knowledge it is capable of storing, and then feed it back to us when we need it.

James Keller, the founder of the Christophers, tells a story in his autobiography *To Light a Candle* *

> I sat next to a scientist at a dinner here in New York. In the course of our conversation I recounted some of the results that had come from the Christ-

* James G. Keller, *To Light a Candle: The Autobiography of James Keller, Founder of the Christophers* (Garden City: Doubleday & Company, Inc., 1963), p. 253.

> opher emphasis on the power and responsibility of each individual. The mere mention of every person's capacity for good brought about an immediate response from him. "You can't miss on this work that you are doing," my dinner companion commented. "Our research has proved that the human mind is capable of storing up ten billion items of information. This means that if a person absorbed twenty-five items every second during an eight hour day, it would take forty years before his brain was filled. In the final analysis, facts themselves show that the stupidest person on the face of the earth is a potential genius.

Just imagine, that brain of ours, if it could talk, could tell us all about hidden talents and traits that have been bouncing around within us, give us the formula for getting them out, and then in a simple, understandable way show us the way to develop those talents.

First, it could tell us what to do first and how to do it.

Second, it could wake us up in the morning with a soft, sweet voice, telling us what an important person we are, direct us throughout the day, and then talk us to sleep at night.

Picture, if you can, a business luncheon. You are taking three prospects to a noonday snack at the club. Two of these gentlemen you met at a golf club, the third at a church bazaar. As you near the entrance to the club, your brain starts to whisper,

> Remember, George and Frank don't drink. Dan does, but he shouldn't. So, stay out of the men's

> grill where the bar is located. Go up to the main dining room. Give your favorite waiter the sign. What sign? Don't you remember the code you worked out with him? Yes, that's it, you say, "Hello Charlie." That's right; as he seats you, you say, "Hello Charlie, what's good today?" Since his name is José, he will start talking about their delicious roast beef and pass up his famous "Will you gentlemen have a cocktail before you order?" Sure he'll remember. I checked with his brain when we walked in.

As the luncheon proceeds, your brain continues to feed you information. It whispers the names and ages of Frank's four children. It reminds you that George is a golf nut and had a hole-in-one at Butterfield last year.

Halfway through the luncheon, you know that you're in like Flynn. Your two jokes went over very big. You are about to tell another story when you hear that inner whisper,

> All right, cut. Be a listener for a while. You know, at times you talk too much. That wife joke of yours, well it's real funny, but you seem to forget that Frank is having trouble with the little lady at home.

As you sign the check, the brain whispers its final bit of advice.

> Order some good cigars. They all enjoy a good smoke after lunch. And one last thing, you know when you're under a little tension your hands

> have a tendency to develop that cold, clammy feeling. So, before you get ready to shake hands goodbye, get out your handkerchief, pretend to be wiping your glasses, but dry off that right hand and give them that firm grip. Hold it for a second. Top it off with your friendly grin, and just a smidgen of a twinkle in those blue eyes of yours. Splendid, splendid. The next time I am going to let you try it all by yourself. Unless you get way out in left field, I won't say a word.

Then there was the suburban housewife. When she was 25 years old she was an executive secretary. She had charm, was personable, and flexible. She not only had unique ideas but got them down on paper. In fact, she had all of her abilities and traits working for her.

But then she got married, and for some unknown reason those abilities and traits that had made her an outstanding executive secretary went back into hiding. She evidently felt that those valuable traits had no place in the life of a wife and a mother.

At the age of 40, she found herself leading a drab life filled with daily routines and problems which confronted the average wife in the community. Her life now became patterned like that of her neighbor, and her neighbor's neighbor.

If her brain could have talked and we could have listened in, we might have heard this:

> So you're having fried chicken again tonight for dinner. Sure, your three boys and your husband like fried chicken, but you have had fried

chicken now three times in the past ten days. Didn't it ever dawn on you that there are other ways to fix chicken? Why not try a baked capon with dressing or a stewed chicken with dumplings?

Sure we're talking about frying chicken, but the same things go for fish. You haven't fixed fish or chicken any other way during the past 12 years, but frying. One would think you were "fry happy." What happened to that unique imagination you had in business? So, you don't seem to have it any more. Oh, you have it all right, but it has grown a bit rusty. Yes, that's what I said, a bit rusty. Anything you do not use becomes rusty, and it does not matter whether it be a muscle, your brain, or your imagination. If you do not use it, that's what happens.

All right, you're willing to listen now, huh? So, we will start with first things first. Get a new cook book. Start trying new ways of fixing the food you think your family likes. Add a few new things to the menu. Now when you serve a meal that the family really "goes for," start your card index system. Write the date, meal served, and what it included. Fill out a new card every time the family likes a new combination that you haven't served before. By the end of the year, you will have a list of menus your family enjoys.

Thumb through this when you are at a loss as to what to cook. You will not only have the answer, but if you have kept these cards up to date, you can tell at a glance how long it has been since you used this combination. Remember every time you use all or a major portion of a combination on a menu card, note the date and mark down what you served, plus anything you might have added. One last thing, how about some red-colored index cards for foods your family dislikes or don't particularly care for.

You like that, huh? O.K., any time you find a certain food someone in the family does not care for, fill out one of the red cards, date it, note where the food was served, whether it was at home, a restaurant, or a friend's house, and how it was prepared; and who in the family didn't like it—O.K.? All right, let's get on to something else.

You have been having trouble lately when your husband has some of his business associates over for dinner or for a few cocktails and a light buffet. Well, you don't have any more trouble than any other wife. Don't you remember last week we talked about not being just another housewife but being the best housewife and the best individual you can be. So, you *do* remember.

How about last Saturday night when you had two couples over for cocktails and dinner? This should have been a breeze, but you had to make a federal case out of it, didn't you? That's what I said a, federal case. And do you know why? Well, I'll tell you.

To begin with, you didn't remember the last time you had these couples in for cocktails, did you? But you did remember you served something that somebody didn't like, and you don't remember what it was or who it was that didn't like it. Oh, you think that maybe it was Mrs. So and So. Wait, wait a minute. You didn't get to be an executive secretary on maybe's, did you? You never told your boss that "Someone called you, and I think it was ———," nor did you tell him, "I made an appointment for you at the club, and I think it was for Tuesday or maybe for Wednesday." And another thing you forgot: what kind of cocktails your friends drank. So you had to store up everything from vodka to sarsaparilla. No wonder you made it a federal case.

And remember the week before at the dance at the Club when you were introduced to two new members and their wives? Your mind was miles away. You were trying to remember whether you told Bob, your oldest son, to let the dog out when he came home; and you were also worrying about the other two—whether or not they were behaving over at the neighbors! Now stop and think. What were the names of the new members you met? Of course, you don't know. You don't even remember what they look like, do you?

Do you know that you could be the most charming and interesting woman in the community, and still be a wonderful wife and good mother? How? Easy. All you have to do is to get out all the abilities and traits that went into hiding when you got married and get them working for you. Then, we do a little thinking, a little planning, and we come up with a program.

Let's start with some of the things you might consider.

One, stop being a martyr for the boys. They're 10, 12, and 14; not 1, 2 and 3.

Two, no more arguments at the dinner table. Set aside a half an hour or an hour for family discussion. Make a game out of it. No one can discuss a subject he hasn't checked out. Dust off the seldom used set of encyclopedias. It could be fun as well as enlightening.

Three, how about jacking up that friendly and happy smile of yours, the smile that used to spring into position automatically—that alluring smile of yours that you now drag out only on occasions.

Sure, you can ask some questions. Go ahead.

Why do you get tired so easy? Don't you really know? You want it straight? You do? You're bored. You're treading water. As I told you before, you do not have a program. Let's start with some of the things you used to do, things that kept you active and interested. Here they are: Exercise—you used to love to take a brisk walk. Now a brisk walk to you is out to the car when it's parked two doors away. And what about golf, bowling and bridge? You were a pretty good competitor, and you enjoyed these too. Now let me give you a rundown on these activities. During the last 24 months, you played two games of golf, no bridge, no bowling. And your total amount of exercise wouldn't have kept your grandmother healthy. And, the legitimate theater—you just didn't get around to making any plans, and when you did, the tickets were all "gulped up" before you decided when you wanted to go and who would go with you. And books—I don't think the three books you read over a two-year period would set any sort of a record.

And what happened to those six hours a week you were going to spend as a volunteer worker at the Rehabilitation Center?

If you're bored, maybe you should start a "Bored Anonymous Club."

So, you're getting mad now. Fine, then I'm getting through, huh? By tomorrow you should be about ready for a complete program. This will include a card index system—one for each of your friends, your husband's friends, and those business prospects you have over for cocktails and dinner. When you finish these cards, they will show what these people drink, what they like to eat, their hobbies, birthdays, anniversaries, etc. You will also have a party card, both for parties you go to and parties you have at home. When you finish these cards, with the information you have gathered and with your new program for living an interesting and useful life, you will find that charming and happy smile of yours will return. One last word, be prepared to be known as the most charming and interesting woman in the community, and not just a suburban woman who has created an image she is trying to live up to.

Then there was also the student. The class had been given the assignment—no less than 1200 words on the subject "Death in the Streets and on the Highways." He was about to start writing when the brain began to talk:

What is your topic? And where are your notes? How much research did you do?

So, you didn't think it was necessary to do any research, and you do not have any notes. And your topic is what—seat belts? Very, very original. Do you know what percentage of your class will write about seat belts? You don't know? Well, I'd say about 75 per cent. Did you have anything else in mind? You did? What? Drunken drivers. Well, that's real original, too. That should pick up another 12 per cent of the class. You also thought of "Excessive Speed On the Highway." Well, that should appeal to another 10 per cent.

Remember the little talk we had some time ago

about "Don't Be Afraid to Be Different?" You do? Well, let's try it here.

Can you think of any one place or places where there actually should never be an accident? You can't? How about intersections of streets, highways, and toll roads that are controlled by stop and go lights? Oh sure, there are accidents there. But why? Yes, that's right. Most accident reports say they are caused by running the red light or jumping the green. But you don't hear much about that unreliable, quick-changing yellow light, do you? Haven't you felt at times it hardly flicks on before you can decide how far from the intersection you are, how fast you are doing, and whether or not you should stop or go through. And while you are trying to decide, that vicious red light flares up in your face and you're in the middle of the intersection. And, remember, you are a young man. You react quickly. You make decisions fast. Now take a person up in years who never was good at making decisions, and who sometimes forgets on which side the brake pedal is located, and we might have a real problem.

Oh no, we don't just start writing. Put the pen down. Let's do a little research first and find out how many accidents occurred last year in the county and city at intersections controlled by stop lights. Find out the time of day or night and weather conditions and the supposed cause of each accident.

When we get this information, we will analyze it. Then we'll do some actual testing on our own. We will take 50 intersections in the city and 25 in the county that are controlled by stop-and-go lights, and time the yellow light. We will then check back and see how the actual timing compares to the time that little yellow light is supposed to stay on. We will also see if all lights are coordinated. Now we're getting some place.

We need one thing more—a suggestion, a solution, a gimmick to wrap up our composition. You have an idea? You do? What is it? A fourth light? An orange light that comes on five seconds before the yellow light. The orange light would let you know that the yellow light was about to flash on, and you wouldn't be so startled or surprised when the yellow light flashed on. Pretty good thinking. It could do the trick. It could prevent a lot of those intersection accidents.

But it has a drawback. It's too costly. It would mean changing or buying millions of new stop lights by every city, county, and state government. But, I think we can get the same result with only a little cost and an educational program.

Before the yellow light flashes on, the green "Go" light blinks 5 times. That lets you know that the yellow light is about to pop up in front of you. You like that, huh? O.K., let's start our research and get all the facts down on paper. Then you're ready to start writing that composition of yours.

The sad part of the story about the executive, the suburban housewife, and the student is: our brain cannot talk, it can't even whisper. It cannot feed back that stored-up information when we need it. We must do all of this by ourselves.

LEARN TO GET ALONG WITH PEOPLE, EVEN THOSE YOU DO NOT LIKE

For some of us this is not easy, but we can do it if we try. I remember my first experience with a person that no one seemed to like. Not having any money, I worked for a year between finishing Quincy High School and entering college. A friend of the family named John Ahern, who was Traffic Manager for the Moorman Manufacturing Company, gave me a job in the shipping department.

John warned me about getting along with the shipping clerk who was a most demanding person. It seemed no one got along with him, so he did not expect me to do any more than try the best I could; and as John said, "I'll try to move you up to the main office as soon as I can."

A lone street car ran out to the edge of town where the plant was located. Its first trip was at 6:30 A.M. for the factory workers, another at 7:30 A.M., and the 8:30 car was for the office workers. I was due on the job at 7:30.

The street car was running a little late my first morning. So, not wanting to be late my first day, I jumped off the street car when it stopped and ran through a railroad siding, then through the plant. I was in the shipping department office when the whistle blew. I thought I had made it until I heard a loud bang of a fist on a desk and a voice with a German accent yelling, "Ven the vistle blows, you be sitting at the desk vorking, not hanging up de coat."

"I ran all the way, sir, from the car line," I said meekly.

"Den you take de 6:30 car," he yelled back.

The third day I had written out some shipping tags. He brought them back and tossed them on my desk. "You finished high school, dat the best you write?" I checked over the tags, then looked up at him and said, "Yes, sir, that's the best I can write."

As the days grew into weeks I began to understand this man. He had no friends. No one tried to understand him. He had a wife who had been sickly for years. He wanted to do a good job. He fought everyone to get things done, and they fought him back.

It was three months later while I was checking a carload of sacks containing sulphur, and the box car was on a siding about three blocks from the plant. It was a hot August day. I had been standing alongside the box car for about an hour when I noticed a small figure walking briskly up the tracks carrying a chair. It was the shipping clerk, and he came up to me and almost smiling, said, "It tis very hot today, maybe you should have a chair to sit on."

When I was transferred upstairs to the Traffic Department, I was the one who several times a day would bring down bills of lading to the shipping department. He never failed to pull up a chair and say, "Sit down and have a little chat and a smoke wit me."

Being young, I never thought much about my relations with Mr. Ziegler, the shipping clerk, but the experience helped me many times in the years that followed. I found that you can get along with most people if you try. And getting along with people is one of the most important ingredients in being successful.

How to get along with people is an individual knack. You must consider your own personality and the person you are dealing with. You should study the other person, his or her likes and dislikes. Learn the other person's habits and idiosyncrasies. Be pleasant; you can still be firm. Be helpful.

THAT BRAIN OF OURS

Since that brain of ours cannot talk, cannot even whisper, and has such an undeveloped capacity, the least we can do is to develop it to be the best pal we ever had. Remember, it will not develop itself. It is something like a bank account. If you do not put something in it, there will be nothing there to draw out when you need it. It has the ability to remember, and also to forget. If you do not train it to help you when you need help, it will act like a stranger when you do. If you do not train it to spell, it will mispell the same word every time. If you do not know the meaning of a new word you have heard or read, and you do not look up the meaning, your brain will not be any help to you the next time that word pops up. If you don't watch it, it will pick up slang, curse words, and slanderous remarks, and skip right over new, meaningful words.

A VOCABULARY FOR THAT IMPORTANT PERSON—YOU

Most of us have a limited vocabulary because we make very little effort to introduce a new word to that marvelous brain of ours. No matter what your status is in life, increasing your vocabulary can be fun. Here is how to do it the easy way.

Every time you hear or read a new word, write it

down. If it is in a book or magazine that is yours, underline it, and put a clip on that page. Each week, pick out five words and look up their meanings. Now get out your tape recorder. This tape is to be labeled, "Me and My Big Words."

On weekends or whenever you have time to put these words on tape, it should sound something like this.

> Hello there, this is Jim Brown [or whoever you are], and his new word program. Here are the five new words for the first week in January:
>
> 1. ESOTERIC, spelled e s o t e r i c, which means sort of secret, or taught to only a select number.
> 2. PERSPICACITY, spelled p e r s p i c a c i t y, meaning the ability to understand, quick sighted.
> 3. ....
> 4. ....
> 5. ....

The second week, or when time is available, you relax, lie back, and play your recording of the week before. Then you add:

> Hello there, this is Jim Brown again, adding five new words to his word program.

Each week relax, lie back, and play the tape from the beginning to where you will add another five words.

By the end of the year, you not only have stored up some 100 new words or more in that brain of yours, but you possibly have improved your spelling and had fun doing it.

If you decide to improve your vocabulary, and do it the easy way as described above, remember:

1. When recording, speak slowly.
2. Enunciate each word distinctly.
3. When you are spelling out each word, pronounce each letter as though it were a separate word.

You know, you might even improve your speaking voice.

THERE ARE NO REAL HANDICAPS

I have known some people who, although almost entirely paralyzed, have from their beds run a most successful business. Every year before Christmas, I receive some Christmas cards from "The Handicapped Artists." Many of these cards were painted by artists who held the brushes between their teeth. When we see what these people can accomplish, we should realize that although some of us do not have all the brain power of others, we can with a little effort, some real desire, and a program, out-distance those who do not have all of their talents and abilities out working for them.

Here is a short program for those who are, or feel they are, handicapped:

1. Find out what others like you are doing.
2. Seek the aid of persons who helped others succeed.
3. Be willing to accept setbacks and have the courage to start over.

4. Work with others, accept their help.
5. Have a program, follow it, and change it when it needs to be changed.

GIVE YOUR BRAIN A REST

Different individuals require differing amounts of rest. When you push that marvelous brain of yours beyond its maximum functioning point, you will accomplish little. *Remember:* When soldiers are marching, they are given a rest period *before* they are tired. Do the same with your brain.

1. Figure out your peak point of "mental alertness." Give your brain a rest before you reach that point.
2. Organize your work so your brain knows what you have in mind.
3. Don't wear it out with unimportant things when you have important matters waiting.
4. Develop it to your fullest capacity. If you do, it will come to your rescue when you need help.

POINTS TO REMEMBER ABOUT IF YOUR BRAIN COULD ONLY TALK

- The human brain is capable of storing huge quantities of information. It is your responsibility to use this power in the most effective way possible.
- Remember the examples of the executive, the suburban housewife, and the student. If their

brains could have talked, they would have immediately been on their way to great success.

- The brain does not develop itself; it is up to the owner of the individual brain to stimulate this development. This development is best carried out by means of a concrete *program.* Why not start your own program now? Start building your vocabulary, for instance, by using the methods suggested in this chapter.
- People have so much unused brain power that a person who delves deeply into his supply can actually surpass in performance other people who have greater potential but do not use it as well.
- Like all the other organs of the body, the brain needs rest. Relax your brain *before* it reaches the state of exhaustion. Follow the program outlined in this chapter for resting your brain.

17

Every Group Needs a Leader

During the world war, a young man asked to be deferred by his draft board because the plant where he worked was engaged in essential war work, and he was the leader of an important unit.

An investigation disclosed he was the leader of the unit, but that there were only two people in the unit—he and his brother-in-law. Unfortunately, the day he came up to be classified, his brother-in-law was home recovering from the flu, and he found himself the leader of a "groupless" unit.

In every community, in every corporation, in every successful venture, there is a leader. Some are natural-born leaders, others cultivate leadership qualities. But regardless, without a leader, no venture will succeed.

If you have ever seen geese in flight, you might have noticed that sometimes they fly in a perfect "V" formation, while at other times they fly in irregular, broken, spread formations. Geese, like people, will not follow a weak leader very long. When the lead goose tires, or is not a strong flyer, the geese will break formation and look for a new leader.

As the geese continue in flight, different ones take over the lead. When a strong flyer is found, the flock will again form behind the leader in a perfect "V" formation.

We have all, at some time or other, been at a meeting, a gathering, or a social event when the success of the whole affair depended upon the person in charge, the chairman, a real leader. Then the leadership changed. The same people were present who attended the last meeting—but what a difference! The chairman of the first meeting had charm; but, more important, he had a program, a program from beginning to end. He refused to allow the meeting to stray down unrelated alleys. He kept the meeting interesting and moving. The new chairman floundered. He did not have a program. The meeting died before it got started.

There is a course in leadership now being offered in several cities. It generally consists of a 3-hour session every week for 7 weeks. Many of the individuals who are enrolled have never spoken before a group before. The classes are limited to about 25. At the first meeting, everyone is asked to get up and talk about himself for two minutes. For many, it is a frightening experience, but they realize that everyone in the class is in the same position, and they are talking about something they know about—themselves.

At the end of the seven-week course, many go back to their unions, their church groups, their political organizations as new individuals, able to stand up and express their feelings. Some are on their way to being leaders of the group.

LEADERS ARE RECOGNIZED FOR WHAT THEY CAN DO

Most leaders get to be leaders because

1. They believe in the program or the venture they are leading.
2. They are willing to spend that extra effort to get things accomplished.
3. They usually have the necessary enthusiasm to inspire others.
4. They not only have the courage of their convictions, but display this courage when others want to quit.
5. They are willing to start over and over again when their aims are not realized.
6. They have the ability to create confidence and are recognized as leaders by what they can do.

LET THE GROUP KNOW YOUR AIMS

If you reach the position of a leader, you will maintain this position much longer if you listen to others; then, formulate your program and let your aims be known. When conditions and circumstances change, have the courage to revise your program. Let those in the group know your reason for the change.

WHEN SPEAKING BEFORE A GROUP, KEEP THE FOLLOWING IN MIND

1. Speak only on subjects you are familiar with.
2. When you know you are to be a speaker, be sure to have a beginning and end to your speech.
3. Don't try to be funny. If you have a humorous incident or a joke, your audience will decide if it is funny.
4. As suggested before, if you have a tape recorder, it will be a great help in practicing your speech. If you want to know what your audience will see and hear, make your final recording before a large mirror.
5. Develop a natural speaking voice. Most people are not impressed by shouting or pounding.
6. Timing and pausing will give you an opportunity to feel the pulse of your audience.
7. Don't ramble.

I had a professor in political science at the University of Illinois who had an unusual gimmick of holding our attention. He continuously scribbled on the blackboard to illustrate his points. When the chalk broke—which was often—he would pick up the small piece from the floor, take careful aim at a partly open window, and let go. Professor Kneer never lost the attention of his students. We were always watching and waiting for the chalk to break and for that uncanny throwing arm to toss that piece of chalk through the 3-inch opening.

One day, my curiosity got the best of me, and I went out between the buildings to the remote area outside of that partly open window. There was at least a two-foot pile of crushed, water-soaked chalk dust, topped off with a hundred or so small bits of chalk. I could only wonder how many thousand hours of attention that chalk pile represented.

DO NOT FOLLOW OLD AND WORN OUT PRACTICES AND POLICIES

Whether you're a leader, a speaker, or a person who is merely expressing an opinion at a meeting, be an individual. Present your ideas in your best individual manner.

Do not try to copy your predecessor, no matter how successful he or she has been.

Do not follow old and accepted practices if you have new, individual ideas that are more practical and more suitable to your personality.

COMPLIMENT OTHERS FOR THEIR IDEAS AND SUGGESTIONS

It is as important to recognize a good idea or a suggestion as to originate it. The combined effort of all individuals toward a successful venture is what is important.

If you give credit where credit is due, you will find that you have established one of the most important ways of having people like you; and being liked by people is one of the first steps toward becoming a leader.

POINTS TO REMEMBER ABOUT LEADING A GROUP

- Remember, there is always a leader behind every successful venture. Many leaders are "naturals," but the qualities of a good leader can be developed.
- Leaders are recognized by their actions—by what they can do. Check out the six characteristics of a good leader outlined in this chapter.
- A leader must be able to express himself to the group. In letting the group know your aims, follow the seven rules in this chapter for speaking as a leader. In general, don't depend on theatrical excesses to assert leadership. Table pounding and excessive levity fail to impress where a sound command of the facts of the situation does.
- Remember, a good leader must be able to stimulate and recognize new and valid ideas. It is not so necessary for a leader to come up with these new ideas himself if he is able to recognize them when others present them.

18

The Ability to Create Will Never Die

Automation may replace the elevator operator—possibly the car attendant, or even that friendly waitress. But the ability to create will never die. If the ability and desire to create should die, we will die with it.

Have you ever studied the face of a five-year-old child on the way home from kindergarten? When that little boy or girl is clutching his or her first attempt in that inspiring world of "Creation"—a crayon colored valentine, an odd shaped heart with irregular printing

L e M m
ov to om y.

on it, you have witnessed a scene that tells a simple story why the ability to create will never die.

The field of creation is unlimited. It can take the form of the smallest and simplest object or the most complex and involved supersonic jet plane. The most important thing about it is that it belongs to the individual, and it can be all-inspiring, gratifying, and uplifting. Individuals who like to create are seldom bored or lonesome.

YOU WILL NEVER KNOW WHETHER YOU CAN CREATE UNTIL YOU TRY

It is not unusual to read about someone who late in life took up a hobby, and the hobby developed into such a successful enterprise that the individual became so well known for the hobby, and no one remembered what his or her life work had been.

Creations generally start with an idea. However, many creations are mere accidents. But, in each case, the individual was attempting to create or do something.

Creating is not limited to physical objects. Creating a new system or a program of operation can be just as important and inspiring. Recently I had lunch with an attorney who was lamenting about the courts in Chicago being five years behind in calling cases up for trial—that he had a personal injury case on the call that was filed six years ago. His problem was trying to refresh the memory of his witnesses as to what happened six years ago. I asked him, "Didn't you take depositions to make a record of their testimony?" "Yes," he replied, "but even after reading to them what they testified to at the time the deposition was taken, they could not remember that they had made the statements contained in the depositions."

After discussing the matter and all of its problems, I got an idea. "Why not make a recording on a small plastic disc of their story in their own words before the depositions are taken, when they are not under tension, and the matter is fresh in their minds. You also can ask leading questions that might be objected to by counsel on the other side when the depositions are taken."

Before we had finished, he added another thought to the suggestion, "I can keep these individual recording discs in the file, but before doing so I am going to make a complete tape recording of all the discs together, along with my personal comments on their testimony and some of the cross examination questions the opposing counsel might ask. Then five or six years later, I will not only have the individual discs to play back for each witness, but I will have my own tape to help me prepare for trial."

One of the most difficult questions to answer is, "What can you do about a person who does not have any ideas, has no enthusiasm, does not want to create anything, and gets mad when you try to help, particularly if that person is your own son or daughter?"

When I hear that question, I always have the feeling that I am trying to answer a question like "How do you catch fish when they are not hungry and refuse to bite?"

Personally I do not think that there is any one answer, or any magic words that will build the fire of enthusiasm under an individual who doesn't want to get out of bed. But I do believe that there are certain basic principles, rules, or guides that can help these reluctant persons to take the first step toward being an individual. To start with, here are a few Don'ts:

First, do not criticize them; it will only make them crawl further back into their shell.
Second, do not try to shame them by pointing out what someone else is doing.
Third, do not threaten them if they do not do something.
Fourth, and most important, do not set goals that are beyond their capacity.

These people who do not have any natural, built-in desire or determination must learn to walk before you can expect them to run. Here are a few suggestions:

1. Compliment them for little things they do.
2. Try to get them to work with others who have desire.
3. Try to arouse their curiosity, then their interest.
4. Try by example to show the gratifying feeling of accomplishment.
5. Do not use the same method or the same person when trying to teach them responsibility, gratitude, and the advantages of being the best individual they can be.

6. Learn their likes and dislikes and build a step-by-step program to create, at first, interest, then desire and enthusiasm.
7. Do not become discouraged with them. They will be the first to notice this and will become more discouraged with themselves.

Many of us have hidden creative abilities, but we have been too busy making a living to recognize or feel the impact of these traits. You will never know your capacity to create until you try.

THE SMALLEST CREATION WILL AFFORD YOU MUCH SATISFACTION

There is a certain satifaction in owning something, solving a problem, or finding a new and quicker way of doing things. This has been a part of our heritage.

Something that belongs to you that you had either a part in creating or the creation of the whole has that something that is a little different, a little extra, from something that you purchased or inherited.

A woman may have the most fascinating hat in the Easter Parade, but if she created, designed, and made that headpiece, it carries a special significance as it nestles atop her head.

ONE CREATION WILL LEAD TO ANOTHER

One of the rewarding things about creating is that it never ends. It is almost like watching the sun rise and set; or, like watching the woodcarver who never seems to finish one carving before he's whittling on the next.

When engaged in creating, whether it be a system, a program, or a new formula, examine all of the possibilities and see where your creation could lead. Do not be afraid to lay aside an idea or a partially completed creation to pick it up at a later date.

MANY CREATIONS ARE THE WORK OF MANY PEOPLE—FIND YOUR PLACE IN THE PROGRAM

You have often heard that teamwork is the best work, or two minds are better than one. Some of our greats in music, in science, in medicine have been the work of two or more. In finding your place in the program keep the following in mind:

1. Find individuals who have the same or like interests or goals.
2. Work with people you believe have ability to contribute to the venture.
3. Gather all of the material you can on the enterprise, both pro and con.
4. Find out what others have done before you, their successes and their failures.
5. Do not try to dominate the group with your opinions.
6. Be flexible. You may have the ability to play various parts in the program.
7. Try to enjoy yourself as the creation takes form.

YOU SHOULD HAVE A COMPLETE IDEA BEFORE YOU BEGIN TO CREATE

You have read this before, but it is so important that it cannot be repeated too much. Some people, however, seem to have the rare ability to proceed with an idea as though they had a built-in program from beginning to end. But these people are few, and most of us should think our ideas through and then reduce our thoughts to a workable outline. Be sure to date it and write your name at the side or bottom of each sheet of paper.

Without a completed idea, most of us will drift off of the course. Having a complete idea will help us in the following ways:

1. We will be able to fit in various pieces as they come to mind, whether they belong in the beginning, middle, or near the end of our workable outline.
2. As we discover new things and change our outline, we have a record of our original thought, plus any changes.
3. Many times we will find that by having a completed idea before we start, we discover pitfalls that should be cleared before we begin.
4. With a completed idea, many times we can determine the following:
   a. Whether our approach and method is the best.
   b. Whether or not we will need outside help or advice.

c. The approximate time necessary for completion.

d. If the idea should develop into something patentable, and later on there is some question whether or not it was your idea, and if so when you developed the item, you have your idea in writing, dated and each page signed.

POINTS TO REMEMBER ABOUT THE ABILITY TO CREATE

- There will always be a place for the creative person. You may have creative talents hidden within you—you will never know if you do or not until you actually try to create.

- Creation has stemmed from conscious development of ideas or even from accidents. In all cases, the creator was trying to *do* something.

- You can help develop creativity in other people, whether they are your friends, employees, or your children. Creativity, however, must always be built upon desire and determination; and developing these qualities, if they are not present, is the first step.

- Being creative is one of the surest ways to gaining satisfaction in your life. Even if your creation isn't earth-shaking, *you* will enjoy it, and *you* will derive satisfaction from it.

- Once you start a program of creativity, you will soon find that one creation will provide the spark for the next.

- Don't waste effort; like other pursuits, creativity demands organization—that is, a program.

19

Why Kill Your Career With Common Mistakes

There are enough hidden and unforeseen problems that will require foresight, individual thinking, and fortitude to reach any goal we set, without stumbling over apparent and common mistakes that have been made by others under the same circumstances.

One of the common mistakes made by many in selecting a life work or a career is to be influenced by someone in their family who would just love to have a doctor, a lawyer, a minister, or a priest whom they could brag about. But these professions are not quite like learning the electric organ in ten simple lessons. Each requires a certain temperment plus years of devoted study, self discipline, and determination.

An accountant who had spent years of study to become a C.P.A. told me this story. He said that he was making a yearly audit of a small corporation for the purpose of filing the company's income tax, when one of the officers of this family-owned company, who spent most of his time on the golf course, asked him to step into his office. When he entered his office this is what the officer said:

> I have been watching you going over our records, and I can see that you have a way with those books. I have always felt that I would be good at that type of work. I was wondering if you would have a morning next week, preferably Tuesday, that we could spend together so you could teach me all about bookkeeping, accounting, and making out one of those so-called Income Tax statements.

Here we have a Certified Public Accountant, who had to study many years and pass a difficult examination in order to get his license, and a young executive who wanted to learn everything there was to learn about accounting on a certain Tuesday morning.

WHETHER IT BE A VOCATION, A PROFESSION, OR A BUSINESS ENTERPRISE, FIND OUT ALL YOU CAN ABOUT IT BEFORE YOU START

As has been stated before, "Do not start running before you have the ball." Which means, do not select a vocation, pick a profession for yourself, or enter a business venture until you have collected all of the possible information that is available. Throughout this book you will read this warning. I feel this advice fits into so many situations that it is well worth repeating.

In business, sometimes we pick up certain expressions, and they become so much a part of us that we do not realize that others might not understand what we mean. I use the expression, *check it out,* in the sense of "finding out all you can about it—then seeing if what you found out is correct." Get all the inside information you can, particularly if it affects any important parts of the proposition.

It never occurred to me that my pet expression "check it out" did not carry the message I hoped it would, until a young man who had finished college and had an appointment for an interview with a large corporation for a job said to me, "I don't understand, sir, about that checking it out you talk about. The only time I have heard this expression is when something like a truck is loaded and ready to roll."

I then realized his father operated a trucking line and that "ready to roll" was an expression familiar to him, and that it might not be understood by a lad whose dad ran a bakery.

So, instead of explaining "check it out" in detail, I suggested we try an experiment. His appointment for the interview was ten days away. During the next week, he was to find out everything about the job, or "position," as he called it, that he could. I would put myself in the same position as though I were to have an interview for the same job. Then three days before the interview, we could get together and check our notes to see how much information we had gathered that would be of help in securing the position.

I didn't tell the young man that I just happened to know some of the top executives of that corporation and was familiar with its operations.

When we met, the young man had "checked it out" as he called it, and this is what he had found out.

First, there were two openings to be filled, one in the drafting department and one in the engineering division of the drafting department.

Second, both positions had a starting salary of $6,700 per year.

Third, the company had the following fringe benefits:

a. Officers stock option plan.
b. Profit-sharing and pension program.
c. Hospitalization and sick leave.
d. Liberal vacation program.
e. Salary and wage program.

Fourth, company stock is listed on the New York Stock Exchange. It had a low of 38½ last year and a high of 46. The company earned $1.68 per share and paid a $1.00 dividend.

After checking over the information the young man had gathered, I opened my file. It was divided into three parts:

1. Data on the personnel manager who would interview the young man.
   a. His name.
   b. His age.
   c. A recent photograph.
   d. He did not finish college.
   e. Started with the company 35 years ago and will retire in five years. (He is against compulsory retirement, but only his wife and a few close friends are aware of his feelings.)
   f. He likes to ask the question rather than have the applicant talk and try to sell himself.
   g. He plays some golf, but his real hobby is fishing. He goes fishing every year in Canada.
   h. He has three children, two daughters and a son. All are married. His son is a lawyer and played football at Michigan. He likes both football and baseball, but he is not a devoted fan.
   i. He lives in the suburbs and commutes by train.
   j. He is a company man and firmly believes in 8 hours of work for 8 hours pay.
   k. He is friendly and likes friendly people; but through years of experience, he can spot a phony a mile away.
   l. He has already reviewed your background and scholastic records. Be governed accordingly.

SUGGESTIONS

When interviewed be sure of the following:

- You are neatly dressed.

- Your fingernails are clean.
- Do not wear a sport coat.
- Wear a hat. For some reason, the interviewer has the feeling that a college graduate who does not wear a hat is not ready to settle down, but is still a "Rah-Rah" boy.

2. You should know something about the company. Here is an outline, details are in the file:
   a. Incorporated in 1905.
   b. Original location.
   c. Present location.
   d. Expansion plan.
   e. Merger being considered with "X" company.
   f. Company policies and programs.
   g. Various departments.
   h. Directors.
   i. Present officers and their backgrounds.
3.
   a. Company products (list in file).
   b. Cities where warehouse and small divisions of company are located.
   c. Sales methods and advertising techniques used.
   d. New products the last few years.
   e. Competitors.
   f. Position of the company in the field with its competitors over the past five years in relation to total sales, profits, and dividends.
   g. Review of company house organ, published every month. (Issues for last twelve months in file.)

After reviewing both our outlines, the young man smiled and said, "I think I know what you mean by checking it out; but to make sure, I would like to review your file over the week-end, you know, just to make sure I don't forget what checking it out means."

BE FACTUAL—NOT EMOTIONAL ABOUT WHAT YOU WANT TO DO

We have talked about individuals who do not seem to have any desire or enthusiasm, who for some reason or another are reluctant to spend any energy to accomplish anything. Now, we go to the other end of the line—those who without reason or cause are ready to join any cause, change jobs when the fancy hits them, and volunteer for anything that sticks its head over the horizon.

If this enthusiasm can be channeled into one or two mainstreams, and not spread all over the river bed, this individual can be a most successful person. It is much easier to train a person not to run until he has the ball than it is to try to persuade a person to take his hands out of his pockets who has no interest in even catching the ball.

A FEW SUGGESTIONS

- Do not be carried away by the glitter of things; get to the real substance.
- If you have to be emotional, be emotional about little or personal matters. Be factual about important things and matters pertaining to business.

• If you find that you have the tendency to start off on a proposition without knowing where it is going, try working with another individual who has the tendency to be overprudent and careful.

• Try getting the proposition down on paper. Make an outline as to what you think it involves, then put it away for a day or two. Take another look at it. You will find that the facts have taken on a firmer look, while the glitter has somewhat faded.

JUST BECAUSE SOMEONE DID IT IN THE PAST DOES NOT MEAN IT WILL BE SUCCESSFUL IN THE FUTURE

Dad's Corner had been a stopping place for motorists for years. But Dad said he was getting old, his health had not been too good, and he would like to have a few years of just fishing and lying around. A check of Dad's books showed he had increased his profits every year for the past ten years, and he had drawn a plan for a motel. The price was right, but there was one hidden fact. Within two years a new highway would bypass Dad's Corner. Whoever bought Dad's Corner wouldn't do enough business to pay the taxes.

Buying a supposedly successful business and then finding out that there was some hidden reason for the owner's wanting to sell, is one of the most common reasons for failure in business.

Another of the most common mistakes is following an old, outdated way of doing something, just because it worked in the past.

Another mistake is often made by individuals who

start a business on a shoestring. They work day and night. Everyone in the family pitches in. They scrape every sugar bowl for working capital. They build the business as though it were a house being built brick by brick. But the average venture that does not have sufficient capital is usually doomed before it gets off of the ground.

There are many mistakes made, because the average person does not recognize the apparent dangers. Here is a list of the most common.

1. Putting someone in charge who is either incompetent, dishonest, or careless.
2. Giving a top position to a member of the family who is not qualified for the job.
3. Plant or factory located in a poor labor market.
4. Poor transportation.
5. No understanding of security measures to protect property and merchandise.
6. Poor or no wage program for employees.
7. Bad packaging or merchandising.
8. Poor communication between management and employees.
9. Inadequate sales program.
10. Inability to change to modern procedures.

DO NOT ENTER ANY ENTERPRISE MERELY BECAUSE SOMEONE THINKS YOU SHOULD

Generally, when you are asked to enter into a business proposition, you are expected to contribute time, money, or know-how; or you have desirable connections. It can be easily understood that if the business venture needs any of the above and you can provide one or more of the missing parts, you are going to be "asked in." Naturally the interested parties are going to show you why, for your own sake, you should enter the enterprise.

Remember this, the bigger the return you are promised, the bigger risk you are probably taking.

Do not enter any enterprise unless—

1. You can afford the money or time.
2. You know the background, ability, and character of the other participants.
3. You have a complete written understanding of:
   a. What each is to contribute.
   b. Amount of liability—whether limited or each is liable for the whole.
   c. Division of profits or stock.
   d. Complete program for operating the business or conducting business.
   e. No oral agreements.
   f. Legal advice before starting.
   g. Advice and suggestions from Certified Accountant as to accounting procedure to be used, plus tax advice.

MAKE YOUR OWN INDIVIDUAL DECISION BASED ON WHAT YOU KNOW

Whether or not you should enter a venture depends to a great deal on whether or not you can afford the time or the money. The final decision should be made by you. It will be your time or your money, or both, that will be at stake. Do not be influenced by what others say, but by what you know.

A person who is in the over-$200,000 wage bracket can take a flyer at drilling an oil well for $10,000 and lose very little. If it comes up dry, well, he is in the 91 per cent income tax bracket on all income over $200,000. And if the well should come up spurting oil, he has a 27 per cent depletion tax advantage—which means in layman terms that 27 per cent of income received from the oil venture is tax free. But, take an individual who makes $15,000 per year. That $10,000 oil-well flyer could mean real trouble for the family if that well came up dry.

So, get all the advice you can about any venture you are planning on entering. Gather all the information available. Determine whether the risk is worth the anticipated results. Be honest with yourself and the facts obtained by you. Then make your decision.

POINTS TO REMEMBER ABOUT AVOIDING COMMON MISTAKES

- There are problems and mistakes that repeatedly and consistently pop up in certain fields. These can be called common mistakes; and these are the ones that are stupid to make. You should make every effort to learn from the mistakes of others when you start a new project.

- Don't allow yourself to be convinced to do something that is against your own best judgment. Too many people have committed serious mistakes by following blindly the well-intentioned advice of family and friends.

- To avoid those common mistakes, find out all about the project or enterprise before you even start it—*check it out.*

- Don't rely blindly on past results. Situations can change fast—especially in our modern, fast-moving world. Also, if you do happen to look to the past results, make sure that they are really the facts and not some interested party's biased version of them.

20

You, the Individual

YOUR INDIVIDUAL PROGRAM

If you have made notes as you browsed through this book, you most likely have a disorganized list of ideas, including do's, don'ts, comments, and a few programs that you started but haven't quite finished.

But whether you made notes or not, you should be aware of one thing—that there is nobody exactly like you in this complicated world we live in. What you are going to do about making yourself the best possible you is now up to you.

For those who have made notes, let's start by doing the following:

First, review your notes and reduce them to an outline form.

Analyze the meaning behind each thought and how it applies to you. Be sure you have noted those hidden talents and abilities hammering within you.

Second, the notes that reflect things you should not do should be turned around to reflect a positive action on your part. For example; "Do not be unfriendly with people you do not like," should be changed to "Develop a friendly smile and attitude; avoid thinking of things you do not like about these individuals; try to understand them; do not engage in any type of argument with them; and try to avoid them when you are not feeling up to par."

Third, when you have analyzed your notes and reduced them to outline form, formulate your own individual program.

Fourth, keep the following in mind:

a. You can do most of the things you want to do.
b. Don't reach for the impossible.
c. Do not be afraid to start over and rewrite your program.
d. You are half-way home when you have thought out a step-by-step program or plan based upon your own individuality.

If you are one of the fortunate ones who have tape recorders and have followed some of the suggestions, you should be ready to review the tapes you made. See if you are satisfied with the tone and quality of your voice, your timing and your phrasing. Have you found any new ways to use your recorder such as to learn a language, to listen to recordings on different ways to succeed, etc.?

Doctors now listen to recordings on what is new in medicine. Some play these recordings while driving to and from the hospital or office. This saves them hours of reading and keeps them abreast of all new and important developments in their profession.

Buy or make your own recordings on ways to improve yourself. I suggest you formulate your own individual program and put it on tape. Be sure your voice reflects enthusiasm. Listen to yourself telling you—that important person, YOU—what you are going to do and how you are going to do it.

In the writing of this book I have tried to limit the use of the word *how*. I personally feel that reading *how* to do this or *how* to do that is not the answer to most of the things we wish to accomplish, but is only the primary step. The next step is to develop the necessary ability and tenacity of purpose, and then formulate a program to fit your own individuality. Having done this, the phrase, "how to do this," can become a reality.

I wish that merely reading how to do things were the answer to all those things we want to do. But I am sure that if I read all that there was to read on how to fly a 707 jet and then announced, "I am ready to solo. Who wants to go along?," I would find "nary" a friend who was interested in flying with me.

So put your thoughts and notes into action. And when you do you will find you are able to accomplish many things that you ordinarily would think of as "not for me."

YOU AND YOUR ANXIETY

In this world of increasing tension, studies show that about 50 per cent of those seeking medical attention find they are suffering from ailments brought about or made worse by anxiety, worry, fear, or emotional stress.

Anxiety in itself is not bad. It can be beneficial. It can be a part of desire, enthusiasm, and success itself. But when it runs amuck, when it creates fear, when it distorts our judgment and affects our normal reactions, it is bad.

If you remember, I took issue with those who write "You can do anything you want to do," and "You can be anything you want to be." I also wrote, "Don't reach for the impossible." One of the myths of today is that you can accomplish anything your little heart desires if you will just try hard enough. This idea may be a popular slogan of a free society, but it is also the forerunner of uncontrolled anxiety. I also wrote that, "I can and you can do most of the things we want to do within our own capacity, and our capacity is much greater than most of us realize."

You have read these words many times as you browsed through this book—FORMULATE A PROGRAM BASED UPON YOUR OWN INDIVIDUALITY. This is an important rule that should be of help to those who find their anxiety all out of proportion when they strive and strive, and have a feeling of guilt when they fail to accomplish something that they never should have attempted in the first place.

If you are one of those individuals whose anxiety is causing you trouble, here are some things for you to check:

1. Do you have a feeling of insecurity? If so, are you doing anything about it besides worrying?
2. Do you worry about things you cannot do anything about?
3. Do you feel inferior to others without any reason?
4. Are you resentful of others who are more successful than you?
5. Do you keep fretting about whether you are doing things right?
6. Are you constantly comparing yourself to others?
7. Do you look for the worst to happen even though it is quite remote?
8. Do you have imaginary illnesses?
9. Do you refuse to listen to reason when your fears or emotional stresses have no sound basis?
10. Do you create dangers that are not real and do not exist?

What can you do about unnatural fears and your overactive anxiety?

First, you must realize and understand that anxiety in itself is not bad.

Second, everyone experiences periods of anxiety in

his or her natural development; it can help self-development and enlarge the scope of activity.

Third, you must learn to understand your anxieties and eliminate the areas that cause unnatural fear.

Fourth, look for what causes the problem and what you can do about it.

Fifth, experience creates confidence, and confidence can dispel unnatural anxiety.

Sixth, you must realize that man is different from other animals because he not only has the capacity to be afraid, but to anticipate and plan. Anxiety is a necessary function of life.

Seventh, do not be afraid or ashamed of your anxiety but formulate a program based upon your own individuality to control those anxieties that are unreal and harmful.

Many times we want to quit, to give up, not knowing that success is so close by. Benjamin Disraeli, a 19th Century British statesman who had the tenacity to keep trying when the average person would have given up long ago, explained his bulldog drive by calling attention to the stonecutter who will hammer away at a rock for perhaps 100 times without a crack showing, and then at the 101st blow it splits in two. It was not the last blow alone that split that rock, but the hundred others that went before.

If you look around you, you will note that people who have a purpose, who are working from a program or plan, who are vitally interested in doing something or helping someone, very seldom have uncontrollable anxiety.

ANOTHER LOOK AT YOUR HUMOR

One of the greatest antibiotics of our times is humor. It can also be classified as a very excellent preventive. It can cure a case of anxiety jitters, reduce out-of-proportion problems to their proper size, make dull things interesting, and turn dreary days into pleasant and delightful mornings, afternoons, and evenings. But humor is very difficult to define. It can range from wit to satire; it can be delicate and refined; or it can be blunt and overpowering.

Humor to each of us is something a little different. As individuals we do not like or enjoy all types of stories or jokes. Many of us have only a slight idea about our own humor and how it affects others as well as ourselves.

We all know individuals who think they are very funny. But thinking you are funny or even being funny is not always humor.

I remember a story about two fellows who were standing in front of a cigar store laughing at a little old lady who had a bit too much to drink and had fallen into the gutter. There she sat in a pool of water, grinning and giggling. A passerby, seeing the little old lady sitting in the gutter and the young men laughing, made this remark, "I wonder how loud you would laugh or how funny this would seem if that were your own mother sitting there in the gutter?"

When the subject of humor is discussed, most people immediately think of being witty, telling jokes, or relating funny incidents, and we must admit that all of these are a part of humor. We also know that the ability to tell a funny story or relate a funny incident is indeed a great asset. But the ability to tell stories and jokes can be a hidden, undiscovered trait just waiting to get out and express itself.

Before getting into developing your ability as a storyteller, let's consider a few Don'ts:

DON'T tell off-color stories in mixed company.

DON'T tell old, worn-out stories.

DON'T tell stories until you have thought out your timing and are sure of the punch line.

DON'T tell a story until you are sure of your audience.

DON'T feel that you must match every story that is told.

DON'T try to compete with those who are unusually gifted storytellers unless you have spent sufficient time and effort in developing your own storytelling technique.

DON'T get the idea that because someone told a story and the story was funny that it will be that funny if you tell it.

DON'T get the idea that you must be telling stories one after another, even though you are a good storyteller.

Now turn these don't around and see how many do's you can make from them.

Let's see what can be done about developing you into a raconteur.

First, get out the tape recorder. If you have a peculiar voice, capitalize on it. If you have a good speaking voice, you might have to develop an unusual twang or nasal tone at times, depending upon the story. Let's see how you sound to yourself on a very simple joke.

> Two drunks were driving along a country road in a driving rain. The driver kept peering through the foggy window. Finally he said,
>
> "Shay, you know what, I shink we are gettin' near a town."
>
> "What makes you shink that?" asked the other drunk.
>
> "We're hittin' more people."

Now this simple story is what I would call a filler story. It should be told after someone has told a drunk story and the laughing has stopped. Then, while there is a pause, the simple joke can be tossed in.

Since we started with a simple drunk joke, here is one that is more involved. See how you sound on the tape recorder telling this story. The spacing between words is for timing. The words underlined are for a rising inflection in your voice. The phrases in quotation marks are to be spoken in an emphatic tone.

> At three o'clock in the morning the phone on the night clerk's desk of a large hotel began to ring. The voice on the other end said:
>
> "Dis is Jim Weedy. I'm wegistered in woom

free-o-free, and I was jest wonderin' what time you're goin' to get that cocktail lounge opin."

"My good man . . . for fifty years we have been opening that cocktail lounge at 8 o'clock in the morning . . . and it will be opened . . . at 8 o'clock."

"In da mornin."

"Yes . . . in the morning."

"Oh tum tum now, let's get it open a wittle earlier, huh?"

"As I said, it will be opened at 8 o'clock . . . as we have done for the past fifty years, and it will . . ."

"Who's your boss?"

"The Night Manager."

"Let me spek to him."

"Night Manager? . . . Dis is Jim Weedy weg-istered in woom free-o-free . . . and I need a wit-tle help in gettin' that cocktail lounge open a wittle earlier than that 8 o'clock."

"My good man . . . the cocktail lounge will not be opened before 8 A.M. . . . But if you are in such *need* of a drink at this hour I will have the bellboy bring you a small bottle of my own per-sonal brand. . . ."

"I'm *not* in no *need* of a drink."

"Then *why* . . . are you so interested in what . . . time we open up the cocktail lounge?"

"I jest woke up . . . and I'm locked up in it."

If you are not a natural-born storyteller, you can develop into a pretty good one if you work with the tape recorder. Let some of your friends listen to your tapes. Be open for suggestions; and, finally, have a good storyteller review your tapes and make suggestions. Try taping jokes and stories that you hear on radio and T.V. Then you try them on the recorder.

I have covered making speeches in another chapter. But remember, funny stories and jokes can make a speech, but be sure that the joke or story fits in with the talk and it is your type of story told in your individual style.

THE ART OF MATURING GRACEFULLY

Accepting realities and the ability to compromise are two of the main ingredients, when mixed properly, that will help create the ability to mature gracefully.

Some of our supposedly great philosophers have written works that give one the impression that we are born to die, that this is a gradual process that starts the day we are born. I say you are born to mature and that this starts with the date of birth.

Since there is no one quite like you, there is no reason why you should not mature in your own individual manner. But how you do it is important. If you are going to fight each phase, if you are going to resent people younger than you and people who are older and can do things you cannot do, you are going to be an unhappy, frustrated, and probably unhealthy person.

I know a charming woman who just turned 40 and is confronted with problems she is not willing to accept. She has known other women who have weathered going through the change of life with ease; why couldn't she? Of course she knew very little about these other women.

Outwardly, the change did not seem to be affecting them.

These women were friendly and kept up their club activities. They played golf. They spent some of their time as nurses' aides in hospitals. They took interesting vacations, and some even went fishing with their husbands. She was sure that these women could not do all these things if they felt like she did.

One day when she was feeling unusually sorry for herself, she said to Gloria, an old friend of hers:

"I wish to hell I was 16 years old again." Gloria, who had known her since she was ten, began to laugh. "Just what is so funny about wanting to be sixteen years old again?"

"You seem to forget I knew you when you were sixteen," Gloria replied.

"So what?"

"Well, I still remember that nasty subject they called algebra and the crying spells you had when those pink and bluish pimples would pop out. And what about those monthly cramps that used to double you up? Have you forgotten about all those things?"

Then they both began to laugh. The more they laughed the funnier it seemed. It almost reached hysterical proportions before they finished.

There are only two types of individuals who mature gracefully, those who come by it naturally and those who understand its problems, its dangers, and do something about them.

I can only make suggestions and tell you about other people. The rest is up to you.

Things I have noticed about people who mature gracefully:

1. They are generally friendly and have a pleasant smile.
2. They like people and enjoy doing things for them.
3. They keep abreast of current events.
4. They do not overdress or try to impress others with their earthly possessions.
5. They are not complainers.
6. They understand people who are younger and people who are older, and have the ability to enjoy both.
7. Those who are fortunate enough to be interested in a sport or sports usually keep that interest throughout life and mature gracefully.
8. Those who are golfers and bowlers and are not hindered by bad health seem to enjoy maturity. A low score in golf or a high score in bowling is a morale lifter and a real thrill. I have some friends who play golf and are in the middle seventies. On occasion, they still shoot their age.

But maturing is not limited to the middle-aged or senior citizen. I stated that it started at birth. And, like the days in the week and the weeks in the month, it moves very slowly.

We go from a baby to a child, and from a child to a teen-ager. Then we pass through that confusing stage when we are trying to find our place in society as a young man or woman. Then on to middle age, and finally to our position as a senior citizen.

I told you in the beginning of this book that you would not be required to fill out any charts or to take any tests, nor would you be graded, classified, or pinned up for inspection. The reason was that I did not want this book to resemble a textbook. There are questions to be answered, but you must ask yourself these questions. So, if you will think of yourself as an individual unlike anyone else, and formulate your own program, based upon your own answers, you should have a program that will help you through the many phases of maturing gracefully.

When I think of maturing gracefully, I always remember a story that a registered nurse told me. Every other Saturday she spent six hours as a volunteer nurse in a senior citizen retirement home.

One Saturday afternoon when she was making her rounds, she stopped by Room 202 where a friendly little lady named Martha lived. When she walked into the room, she noticed falsies hanging in the window. She didn't mention what she saw until she was about to leave. Then very casually she said, "Are those your falsies, Martha, drying out over there?" Martha looked around as though she hadn't the slightest idea of what might be hanging over there. "In the window, Martha."

"Oh, in the window," Martha repeated. "Well, you see," she started timidly, "I have a new cashmere sweater, and these very nice people are taking me out to dinner tonight. They take me out for dinner every month, and we always have a couple of drinks before we dine, and I like dry manhattans. I enjoy these evenings so much."

"But what goes with the falsies?" the nurse asked.

"Well, I just don't think that a cashmere sweater looks like it should if it don't have a couple of things pushing out in front, and at my age I just don't have anything pushing out there in front."

When I think of maturing gracefully I always think of Martha, because the little lady with the cashmere sweater was 95 years old.

HOW TO WIND UP YOUR DAY

As you start to wind up your day, you should start to unwind yourself. Whether you be a student, a worker, or an executive, there comes a time each day when you must call it quits. As you approach that time, you should have your own relaxing routine.

You will never relax if you leave unfinished business without a program for completing this unfinished work the next day.

Have you ever watched a painter as he nears the end of a working day when he realizes he cannot finish the room he has been painting? He starts to wind up his day by soaking his brushes and stirring his paints. If he has several rooms to paint, he might mix some to match the color chart for these rooms. When he leaves, if he is an experienced painter, everything is in order for the next day. His brushes are clean and dry. His paints have been blended and stored in tight cans. He has checked all his other equipment and put it in order. He has not only wound up his working day, but he has everything organized for the day to come.

Actually, there are two parts to winding up the day: one from the daily routine, your work; and the other as you approach your bedtime. The latter was discussed in a previous chapter.

No matter what I write or how many suggestions I make, if you are not interested in working out a program for yourself based on what you know about yourself and your own individuality, you will find yourself fighting the end of the day and hating the day to come.

I know an old fishing guide who lives in the northwoods. His deeply wrinkled, bronze face and deep-set, squinting eyes tell the story of subzero winters and the bright summer sun. No one knows where old John came from or how old he is. But he never failed to give his best for that fisherman who came north each summer to catch fish. He had little "gimmicks," like sunken sacks of old bread that he sank off a sandbar, and personal hidden brush piles of his own that he had sunk in certain spots. He never sunk one without wiring 10 or 15 banana stalks to the lower limbs. Whether or not the fish like to hang around John's secret spots I don't know, but he usually comes in with a grin, a twinkle in those deep set eyes, and a string of fish.

John could clean and pack fish in ice faster than anyone I knew. Then, when he had been paid and the fishermen were on their way, he started winding up his day.

First, he checked his lines and fishing gear.

Second, he took another look at his box of hooks, sinkers, plugs, and spoons.

Third, he checked his minnow trap and minnow box. He also looked in on the few live frogs he kept.

Fourth, he cleaned out his boat and checked the motor. He checked his gas supply.

Fifth, some days just before dark he would go out and move those sunken sacks of bread to a new location. Experience had taught old John that there were all types of fishermen just like there were all types of people, and there were always a few that thought they knew the hot fishing spots and would not need John's services two days later when they planned to fish that lake again.

Sixth, when he was sure that everything was in order for the next day, he generally took a quick dip or a shower. Then, with a bottle of beer and his pipe he listened to the radio for the weather forecast for the next day.

He usually cooked his own meals; but if he wasn't booked for the next day, he would go up to the village or the county tavern. Here he would meet new fishermen and some of the friends he had known for years. He had that unique ability of telling fish stories that led you to believe he could talk to fish, and that they were just waiting to be caught by the fishermen that John guided.

Before going to bed he always read something from

the Bible to wind up his day. Then he was off to that peaceful night of sleep he felt he had earned.

John was indeed an individual. He not only had a program for his work and for winding up his day, but he evidently gave thought to winding up his life. For on the wall in his small cabin hung a wooden plaque with a poem burned into the wood. Who the author was I do not know, but here is how it read:

GOD GRANT THAT I MAY LIVE TO FISH
UNTO MY DYING DAY
AND WHEN IT COMES TO MY LAST CAST
I THEN MOST HUMBLY PRAY
WHEN IN THE LORD'S LANDING NET
I'M PEACEFULLY ASLEEP
THAT IN HIS MERCY I BE JUDGED
GOOD ENOUGH TO KEEP.